Odoo Development Essentials

Fast track your development skills to build powerful
Odoo business applications

Daniel Reis

[PACKT] open source *
PUBLISHING
community experience distilled

BIRMINGHAM - MUMBAI

Odoo Development Essentials

First published: April 2015

Production reference: 2090615

Published by Packt Publishing Ltd.
Livery Place
35 Livery Street
Birmingham B3 2PB, UK.

ISBN 978-1-78439-279-6

www.packtpub.com

Credits

Author
Daniel Reis

Reviewers
Pedro M. Baeza
Nicolas Bessi
Alexandre Fayolle

Commissioning Editor
Amarabha Banerjee

Acquisition Editor
Subho Gupta

Content Development Editor
Siddhesh Salvi

Technical Editors
Ankur Ghiye
Manali Gonsalves
Naveenkumar Jain

Copy Editors
Hiral Bhat
Pranjali Chury
Wishva Shah
Sameen Siddiqui

Project Coordinator
Nidhi J. Joshi

Proofreaders
Paul Hindle
Chris Smith

Indexer
Tejal Soni

Production Coordinator
Nilesh R. Mohite

Cover Work
Nilesh R. Mohite

About the Author

Daniel Reis has worked in the IT industry for over 15 years, most of it for a multinational consultancy firm, implementing business applications for a variety of sectors, including telco, banking, and industry. He has been working with Odoo (formerly OpenERP) since 2010, is an active contributor to the Odoo Community Association projects, and has been a regular speaker at the OpenDays annual conference.

He currently works at Securitas, a global security services company, where he introduced Python and Odoo into the applications portfolio.

About the Reviewers

Pedro M. Baeza is an Odoo freelance consultant, developer, and trainer with more than 16 years of experience in IT. He's been in the Odoo world for 4 years, and has been involved in its community since the beginning, first in the Spanish community, and then in the worldwide community that later formed the Odoo Community Association (OCA). Currently, he is the Spanish localization PSC and website PSC team leader, and also an active reviewer and contributor for most of the community projects.

He doesn't have direct employees, but collaborates with other companies and freelancers to deploy Odoo implementations. He feels that the best part of this is having to contact a lot of awesome people to work with to get to a common goal and that this is the perfect environment for getting close to perfection!

I would like to thank the awesome community, which is spread around the world, for pushing me a little further and adding to my knowledge. I also want to thank my girlfriend (and future wife), Esther, for understanding why I'm unable to spend time with her because of the job and my current commitment to the community.

Nicolas Bessi has been an Odoo/OpenERP developer and consultant since 2006 when it was still TinyERP. He is the author of many modules including the "report webkit" add-on that was part of the official add-ons for many years, which inspired the actual QWeb report engine.

He's an active member of Odoo Community Association and is responsible for Swiss localization. He was recognized as an OpenERP top contributor in 2010, and is still an active partisan of Open Source values.

Nicolas is a technical leader at Camptocamp, a leading society in Open Source technologies that is a historical Odoo contibutor and partner. Camtocamp is actively working alongside Odoo to bring the solution to the next level.

Alexandre Fayolle installed his first Linux distribution in 1995 (Slackware at the time, before moving to Debian in 1996) and has never used another OS on his computers since. He started using Python in 1999 when he cofounded Logilab, where he was a CTO, software architect, and Agile coach. He got the opportunity to participate in a large number of FLOSS projects, including pyxml, Pypy, Cubicweb, and Pylint. In 2012, he joined Camptocamp to work on Odoo, which was still called OpenERP at the time. He became a very active member of the Odoo Community Association, both as a direct module contributor and as a mentor to new comers. He also happens to be a jazz vibraphone player.

www.PacktPub.com

Support files, eBooks, discount offers, and more

For support files and downloads related to your book, please visit www.PacktPub.com.

Did you know that Packt offers eBook versions of every book published, with PDF and ePub files available? You can upgrade to the eBook version at www.PacktPub.com and as a print book customer, you are entitled to a discount on the eBook copy. Get in touch with us at service@packtpub.com for more details.

At www.PacktPub.com, you can also read a collection of free technical articles, sign up for a range of free newsletters and receive exclusive discounts and offers on Packt books and eBooks.

https://www2.packtpub.com/books/subscription/packtlib

Do you need instant solutions to your IT questions? PacktLib is Packt's online digital book library. Here, you can search, access, and read Packt's entire library of books.

Why subscribe?

- Fully searchable across every book published by Packt
- Copy and paste, print, and bookmark content
- On demand and accessible via a web browser

Free access for Packt account holders

If you have an account with Packt at www.PacktPub.com, you can use this to access PacktLib today and view 9 entirely free books. Simply use your login credentials for immediate access.

Table of Contents

Preface

Odoo is a powerful open source platform for business applications. On top of it a suite of closely integrated applications was built, covering all business areas from CRM and Sales to Accounting and Stocks. Odoo has a dynamic and growing community around it, constantly adding features, connectors, and additional business apps.

Odoo Development Essentials provides a step-by-step guide to Odoo development to quickly climb the learning curve and become productive in the Odoo application platform.

The first three chapters aim to make the reader comfortable with Odoo, the basic techniques to set up a development environment, and with the module development approach and workflow.

The next five chapters explain in detail several development areas used in modules: data files, models, views, business logic, and QWeb.

The two final chapters guide you through integrating Odoo applications with external applications and discuss what to consider when deploying your Odoo instance for production use.

What this book covers

Chapter 1, Getting Started with Odoo Development, covers setting up a development environment, installing Odoo from source, and learning how to manage Odoo server instances.

Chapter 2, Building Your First Odoo Application, guides you through the creation of your first Odoo module, covering all the different layers involved: models, views, and business logic.

Chapter 3, Inheritance – Extending Existing Applications, explains the inheritance mechanisms and uses them to create extension modules that add or modify features on other existing modules.

Chapter 4, Data Serialization and Module Data, covers the most used Odoo data file formats, XML and CSV, external identifiers, and how to use data files in modules and in data import/export.

Chapter 5, Models – Structuring the Application Data, discusses in detail the Model layer with the types of models and fields available, including relational and computed fields.

Chapter 6, Views – Designing the User Interface, covers the View layer, explaining in detail several types of views and all the elements that can be used to create dynamic and intuitive user interfaces.

Chapter 7, ORM Application Logic – Supporting Business Processes, introduces programming business logic on the server side, exploring the ORM concepts and features, and also explains how to use wizards for sophisticated user interaction.

Chapter 8, QWeb – Creating Kanban Views and Reports, goes over the Odoo QWeb templates, using them to create rich kanban boards and HTML-based reports.

Chapter 9, External API – Integration with Other Systems, explains how to use Odoo server logic from external applications, and introduces a popular client programming library that can also be used as a command-line client.

Chapter 10, Deployment Checklist – Going Live, shows you how to prepare a server for production prime time and explains what configuration should be taken care of and how to configure an Nginx reverse proxy for improved security and scalability.

What you need for this book

We will install our Odoo server in an Ubuntu or Debian system, but we expect you to use the operating system and programming tools of your choice, be it Windows, Macintosh, or any other.

We will provide some guidance on setting up a virtual machine with Ubuntu Server. You should choose the virtualization software to be used, such as VirtualBox or VMware Player, both available for free. If you are using Ubuntu or Debian workstation, no virtual machine will be needed.

Who this book is for

This book is targeted at developers with experience in developing business applications who are willing to quickly become productive with Odoo.

You are expected to have an understanding of MVC application design and knowledge of the Python programming language.

Conventions

In this book, you will find a number of styles of text that distinguish between different kinds of information. Here are some examples of these styles, and an explanation of their meaning.

Code words in text, database table names, folder names, filenames, file extensions, pathnames, dummy URLs, user input, and Twitter handles are shown as follows: "It also needs to be Python importable, so it must also have a __init__.py file."

A block of code is set as follows:

```
{
    'name': 'To-Do Application',
    'description': 'Manage your personal Tasks with this module.',
    'author': 'Daniel Reis',
    'depends': ['mail'],
    'application': True,
}
```

Any command-line input or output is written as follows:

```
$ mkdir ~/odoo-dev/custom-addons
```

New terms and **important words** are shown in bold. Words that you see on the screen, in menus or dialog boxes for example, appear in the text like this: "Select the **Update Modules List** option."

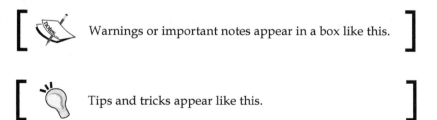

Warnings or important notes appear in a box like this.

Tips and tricks appear like this.

Reader feedback

Feedback from our readers is always welcome. Let us know what you think about this book—what you liked or may have disliked. Reader feedback is important for us to develop titles that you really get the most out of.

To send us general feedback, simply send an e-mail to feedback@packtpub.com, and mention the book title via the subject of your message.

If there is a topic that you have expertise in and you are interested in either writing or contributing to a book, see our author guide on www.packtpub.com/authors.

Customer support

Now that you are the proud owner of a Packt book, we have a number of things to help you to get the most from your purchase.

Downloading the example code

You can download the example code files for all Packt books you have purchased from your account at http://www.packtpub.com. If you purchased this book elsewhere, you can visit http://www.packtpub.com/support and register to have the files e-mailed directly to you.

Errata

Although we have taken every care to ensure the accuracy of our content, mistakes do happen. If you find a mistake in one of our books—maybe a mistake in the text or the code—we would be grateful if you would report this to us. By doing so, you can save other readers from frustration and help us improve subsequent versions of this book. If you find any errata, please report them by visiting http://www.packtpub.com/submit-errata, selecting your book, clicking on the **errata submission form** link, and entering the details of your errata. Once your errata are verified, your submission will be accepted and the errata will be uploaded on our website, or added to any list of existing errata, under the Errata section of that title. Any existing errata can be viewed by selecting your title from http://www.packtpub.com/support.

Piracy

Piracy of copyright material on the Internet is an ongoing problem across all media. At Packt, we take the protection of our copyright and licenses very seriously. If you come across any illegal copies of our works, in any form, on the Internet, please provide us with the location address or website name immediately so that we can pursue a remedy.

Please contact us at copyright@packtpub.com with a link to the suspected pirated material.

We appreciate your help in protecting our authors, and our ability to bring you valuable content.

Questions

You can contact us at questions@packtpub.com if you are having a problem with any aspect of the book, and we will do our best to address it.

1
Getting Started with Odoo Development

Before we dive into Odoo development, we need to set up our development environment, and you need to learn the basic administration tasks for it.

In this chapter, you will learn how to set up the work environment, where we will later build our Odoo applications.

You will also learn how to set up a Debian or Ubuntu system to host our development server instances, and how to install Odoo from the GitHub source code. Then you will learn how to set up file sharing with Samba, allowing you to work on Odoo files from a workstation running Windows or any other operating system.

Odoo is built using the Python programming language and uses the PostgreSQL database for its data storage, so these are the main requirements we should have in our Odoo host.

To run Odoo from source, we will need to install first the Python libraries it depends on. The Odoo source code can then be downloaded from GitHub and executed from source. While we can download a zip or tarball, it's best to get the sources using GitHub, so we'll also have it installed on our Odoo host.

Setting up a host for the Odoo server

We will prefer using Debian/Ubuntu for our Odoo server, even though you will still be able to work from your favorite desktop system, be it Windows, Macintosh, or Linux.

Odoo can run on a variety of operating systems, so why pick Debian at the expense of other operating systems? Because Odoo is developed primarily with the Debian/Ubuntu platform in mind, it supports Odoo better. It will be easier to find help and additional resources if working with Debian/Ubuntu.

It's also the platform the majority of developers work on, and where most deployments are rolled out. So, inevitably, Odoo developers will be expected to be comfortable with that platform. Even if you're from a Windows background it will be important to have some knowledge about it.

In this chapter, you will learn how to set up and work with Odoo hosted in a Debian system, using only the command line. For those more at home with a Windows system, we will cover how to set up a virtual machine to host the Odoo server. As a bonus, the techniques you will learn will also allow you to manage Odoo in cloud servers where your only access will be through **Secure Shell (SSH)**.

 Keep in mind that these instructions are intended to set up a new system for development. If you want to try some of them in an existing system, always take a backup ahead of time to be able to restore it in case something goes wrong.

Provisions for a Debian host

As explained earlier, we will need a Debian host for our Odoo version 8.0 server. If these are your first steps with Linux, you may like to know that Ubuntu is a Debian-based Linux distribution, so they are very similar.

 Odoo is guaranteed to work with the current stable version of Debian or Ubuntu. At the time of writing this book, these are Debian 7 "Wheezy" and Ubuntu 14.04 "Trusty Tahr". Both ship with Python 2.7, necessary to run Odoo.

If you are already running Ubuntu or another Debian-based distribution, you're set; this machine can also be used as a host for Odoo.

For the Windows and Macintosh operating systems, it is possible to have Python, PostgreSQL, and all the dependencies installed, and then run Odoo from source natively.

However, that could prove to be a challenge, so our advice is to use a virtual machine running Debian or Ubuntu Server. You're welcome to choose your preferred virtualization software to get a working Debian system in a VM. If you need some guidance, here is some advice: regarding the virtualization software, you have several options, such as Microsoft Hyper-V (available in some versions of Windows), Oracle VirtualBox, or VMWare Player (or VMWare Fusion for Macintosh). VMWare Player is probably easier to use, and free-to-use downloads can be found at https://my.vmware.com/web/vmware/downloads.

Regarding the Linux image to use, Ubuntu Server is more user friendly to install than Debian. If you're beginning with Linux, I would recommend trying a ready-to-use image. TurnKey Linux provides easy-to-use, preinstalled images in several formats, including ISO. The ISO format will work with any virtualization software you choose, or even on a bare-metal machine you might have. A good option might be the LAPP image, found at http://www.turnkeylinux.org/lapp.

Once installed and booted, you should be able to log in to a command-line shell.

If you are logging in using root, your first task should be to create a user to use for your work, since it's considered bad practice to work as root. In particular, the Odoo server will refuse to run if you are using root.

If you are using Ubuntu, you probably won't need this since the installation process has already guided you in the creation of a user.

Creating a user account for Odoo

First, make sure sudo is installed. Our work user will need it. If logged in as root:

```
# apt-get update && apt-get upgrade  # Install system updates
# apt-get install sudo  # Make sure 'sudo' is installed
```

The following commands will create an odoo user:

```
# useradd -m -g sudo -s /bin/bash odoo  # Create an 'Odoo' user with sudo powers
# passwd odoo  # Ask and set a password for the new user
```

You can change odoo to whatever username you want. The -m option has its home directory created. The -g sudo adds it to the sudoers list, so it can run commands as root, and the -s /bin/bash sets the default shell to bash, which is nicer to use than the default sh.

Now we can log in as the new user and set up Odoo.

Installing Odoo from source

Ready-to-install Odoo packages can be found at `nightly.odoo.com`, available as Windows (`.exe`), Debian (`.deb`), CentOS (`.rpm`), and source code tarballs (`.tar.gz`).

As developers, we will prefer installing directly from the GitHub repository. This will end up giving us more control over versions and updates.

To keep things tidy, let's work in an `/odoo-dev` directory inside your home directory. Throughout the book, we will assume this is where your Odoo server is installed.

First, make sure you are logged in as the user created above, or during the installation process, and not as root. Assuming your user is `odoo`, you can confirm this with the following command:

```
$ whoami

odoo

$ echo $HOME

/home/odoo
```

Now we can use this script. It shows us how to install Odoo from source in a Debian system:

```
$ sudo apt-get update && sudo apt-get upgrade  # Install system updates
$ sudo apt-get install git  # Install Git
$ mkdir ~/odoo-dev  # Create a directory to work in
$ cd ~/odoo-dev  # Go into our work directory
$ git clone https://github.com/odoo/odoo.git -b 8.0  # Get Odoo source
code
$ ./odoo/odoo.py setup_deps  # Installs Odoo system dependencies
$ ./odoo/odoo.py setup_pg  # Installs PostgreSQL & db superuser for unix
user
```

At the end, Odoo should be ready to be used. The ~ symbol is a shortcut for your home directory (for example, `/home/odoo`). The `git -b 8.0` option asks to explicitly download the 8.0 branch of Odoo. At the time of writing this book, this is redundant, since 8.0 is the default branch, but this may change, so it will make the script time resilient.

To start an Odoo server instance, just run `odoo.py`:

```
$ ~/odoo-dev/odoo/odoo.py
```

By default, Odoo instances listen from port 8069, so if we point a browser to
`http://<server-address>:8069` we will reach that instance. When we are
accessing it for the first time, it will show us an assistant to create a new database,
as shown in the following screenshot:

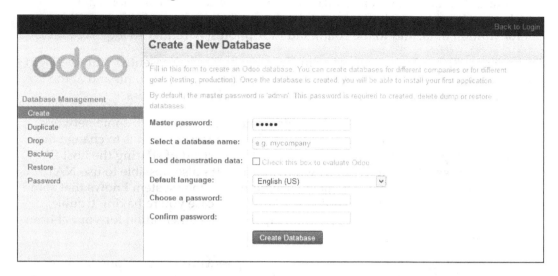

But we will learn how to initialize new databases from the command line, now so
press *Ctrl + C* to stop the server and get back to the command prompt.

Initializing a new Odoo database

To be able to create a new database, your user must be a PostgreSQL superuser.
The `./odoo.py setup_pg` does that for you; otherwise use the following command
to create a PostgreSQL superuser for the current Unix user with:

```
$ sudo createuser --superuser $(whoami)
```

To create a new database we use the command `createdb`. Let's create a `v8dev`
database:

```
$ createdb v8dev
```

To initialize this database with the Odoo data schema we should run Odoo on the
empty database by using the `-d` option:

```
$ ~/odoo-dev/odoo/odoo.py -d v8dev
```

This will take a couple of minutes to initialize a v8dev database, and will end with an INFO log message **Modules loaded**. Then the server will be ready to listen to client requests.

By default, this method will initialize the database with demonstration data, which often is useful on development databases. To initialize a database without demonstration data, add to the command the option: --without-demo-data=all.

Open http://<server-name>:8069 in your browser to be presented with the login screen. If you don't know your server name, type the hostname command at the terminal to find it, or the ifconfig command to find the IP address.

If you are hosting Odoo in a virtual machine you might need to do some network configuration to be able to use it as a server. The simplest solution is to change the VM network type from NAT to Bridged. With this, instead of sharing the host IP address, the guest VM will have its own IP address. It's also possible to use NAT, but that requires you to configure port forwarding, so your system knows that some ports, such as 8069, should be handled by the VM. In case you're having trouble, hopefully these details can help you find help in the documentation for your chosen virtualization software.

The default administrator account is admin with password admin. Upon login you are presented with the **Settings** menu, displaying the installed modules. Remove the **Installed** filter and you will be able to see and install any of the official modules.

Whenever you want to stop the Odoo server instance and return to the command line, press *Ctrl + C*. At the bash prompt, pressing the Up arrow key will bring you the previous shell command, so it's a quick way to start Odoo again with the same options. You will see the *Ctrl + C* followed by Up arrow and *Enter* is a frequently used combination to restart the Odoo server during development.

Managing your databases

We've seen how to create and initialize new Odoo databases from the command line. There are more commands worth knowing for managing databases.

You already know how to use the createdb command to create empty databases, but it can also create a new database by copying an existing one, by using a --template option.

Make sure your Odoo instance is stopped and you have no other connection open on the v8dev database created above, and run:

```
$ createdb --template=v8dev v8test
```

In fact, every time we create a database, a template is used. If none is specified, a predefined one called `template1` is used.

To list the existing databases in your system use the PostgreSQL utility `psql` utility with the `-l` option:

```
$ psql -l
```

Running it we should see listed the two databases we created so far: `v8dev` and `v8test`. The list will also display the encoding used in each database. The default is UTF8, which is the encoding needed for Odoo databases.

To remove a database you no longer need (or want to recreate), use the `dropdb` command:

```
$ dropdb v8test
```

Now you know the basics to work with several databases. To learn more on PostgresSQL, the official documentation can be found at `http://www.postgresql.org/docs/`

 WARNING: The drop database will irrevocably destroy your data. Be careful when using it and always keep backups of your important databases before using it.

A word about Odoo product versions

At the date of writing, Odoo's latest stable is version 8, marked on GitHub as branch 8.0. This is the version we will work with throughout the book.

It's important to note that Odoo databases are incompatible between Odoo major versions. This means that if you run Odoo 8 server against an Odoo/OpenERP 7 database, it won't work. Non-trivial migration work is needed before a database can be used with a later version of the product.

The same is true for modules: as a general rule a module developed for an Odoo major version will not work with other versions. When downloading a community module from the Web, make sure it targets the Odoo version you are using.

On the other hand, major releases (7.0, 8.0) are expected to receive frequent updates, but these should be mostly fixes. They are assured to be "API stable", meaning that model data structures and view element identifiers will remain stable. This is important because it means there will be no risk of custom modules breaking due to incompatible changes on the upstream core modules.

And be warned that the version in the master branch will result in the next major stable version, but until then it's not "API stable" and you should not use it to build custom modules. Doing so is like moving on quicksand: you can't be sure when some changes will be introduced that will make you custom module break.

More server configuration options

The Odoo server supports quite a few other options. We can check all available options with the `--help` option:

```
$ ./odoo.py --help
```

It's worth while to have an overview on the most important ones.

Odoo server configuration files

Most of the options can be saved in a configuration file. By default, Odoo will use the `.openerp-serverrc` file in your home directory. Conveniently, there is also the `--save` option to store the current instance configuration into that file:

```
$ ~/odoo-dev/odoo/odoo.py --save --stop-after-init  # save configuration
to file
```

Here we also used the `--stop-after-init` option, to have the server stop after it finishes its actions. This option is often used when running tests or asking to run a module upgrade to check if it installs correctly.

Now we can inspect what was saved in this default configuration file:

```
$ more ~/.openerp_serverrc  # show the configuration file
```

This will show all configuration options available with the default values for them. Editing them will be effective the next time you start an Odoo instance. Type q to quit and go back to the prompt.

We can also choose to use a specific configuration file, using the `--conf=<filepath>` option. Configuration files don't need to have all those the options you've just seen. Only the ones that actually change a default value need to be there.

Changing the listening port

The `--xmlrpc-server=<port>` command allows us to change the default 8069 port where the server instance listens. This can be used to run more than one instances at the same time, on the same server.

Let's try that. Open two terminal windows. On the first one run:

```
$ ~/odoo-dev/odoo.py --xmlrpc-port=8070
```

and on the other run:

```
$ ~/odoo-dev/odoo.py --xmlrpc-port=8071
```

And there you go: two Odoo instances on the same server listening on different ports. The two instances can use the same or different databases. And the two could be running the same or different versions of Odoo.

Logging

The `--log-level` option allows us to set the log verbosity. This can be very useful to understand what is going on in the server. For example, to enable the debug log level use: `--log-level=debug`

The following log levels can be particularly interesting:

- `debug_sql` to inspect SQL generated by the server
- `debug_rpc` to detail the requests received by the server
- `debug_rpc_answer` to detail the responses sent by the server

By default the log output is directed to standard output (your console screen), but it can be directed to a log file with the option `--logfile=<filepath>`.

Finally, the `--debug` option will bring up the Python debugger (`pdb`) when an exception is raised. It's useful to do a post-mortem analysis of a server error. Note that it doesn't have any effect on the logger verbosity. More details on the Python debugger commands can be found here: `https://docs.python.org/2/library/pdb.html#debugger-commands`.

Developing from your workstation

You may be running Odoo with a Debian/Ubuntu system, either in a local virtual machine or in a server over the network. But you may prefer to do the development work in your personal workstation, using your favorite text editor or IDE.

This may frequently be the case for developers working from Windows workstations. But it also may be the case for Linux users that need to work on an Odoo server over the local network.

A solution for this is to enable file sharing in the Odoo host, so that files are easy to edit from our workstation. For Odoo server operations, such as a server restart, we can use an SSH shell (such as PuTTY on Windows) alongside our favorite editor.

Using a Linux text editor

Sooner or later, we will need to edit files from the shell command line. In many Debian systems the default text editor is `vi`. If you're not comfortable with it, then you probably could use a friendlier alternative. In Ubuntu systems the default text editor is `nano`. You might prefer it since it's easier to use. In case it's not available in your server, it can be installed with:

```
$ sudo apt-get install nano
```

In the following sections we will assume `nano` as the preferred editor. If you prefer any other editor, feel free to adapt the commands accordingly.

Installing and configuring Samba

The Samba project provides Linux file sharing services compatible with Microsoft Windows systems. We can install it on our Debian/Ubuntu server with:

```
$ sudo apt-get install samba samba-common-bin
```

The `samba` package installs the file sharing services and the `samba-common-bin` package is needed for the `smbpasswd` tool. By default users allowed to access shared files need to be registered with it. We need to register our user `odoo` and set a password for its file share access:

```
$ sudo smbpasswd -a odoo
```

After this the `odoo` user will be able to access a fileshare for its home directory, but it will be read only. We want to have write access, so we need to edit Sambas, configuration file to change that:

```
$ sudo nano /etc/samba/smb.conf
```

In the configuration file, look for the `[homes]` section. Edit its configuration lines so that they match the settings below:

```
[homes]
    comment = Home Directories
    browseable = yes
    read only = no
    create mask = 0640
    directory mask = 0750
```

For the configuration changes to take effect, restart the service:

```
$ sudo /etc/init.d/smbd restart
```

> **Downloading the example code**
>
> You can download the example code files for all Packt books you have purchased from your account at http://www.packtpub.com. If you purchased this book elsewhere, you can visit http://www.packtpub.com/support and register to have the files e-mailed directly to you.

To access the files from Windows, we can map a network drive for the path \\<my-server-name>\odoo using the specific user and password defined with smbpasswd. When trying to log in with the odoo user, you might find trouble with Windows adding the computer's domain to the user name (for example MYPC\odoo). To avoid this, use an empty domain by prepending a \ to the login (for example \odoo).

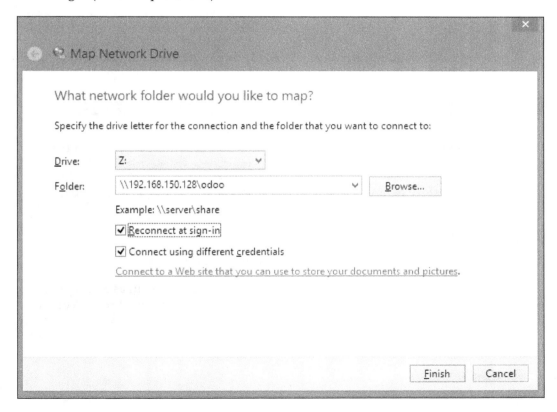

If we now open the mapped drive with Windows Explorer, we will be able to access and edit the contents of the odoo user home directory.

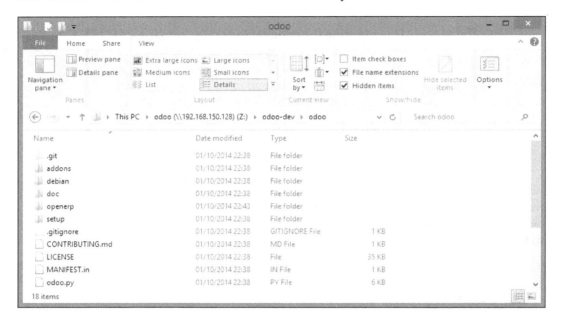

Enabling the on-board technical tools

Odoo includes some tools that are very helpful for developers, and we will make use of them throughout the book. They are the Technical Features and the Developer Mode.

These are disabled by default, so this is a good moment to learn how to enable them.

Activating the Technical Features

Technical Features provide advanced server configuration tools.

They are disabled by default, and to enable them, we need to log in as admin. In the **Settings** menu, select **Users** and edit the Administrator user. In the **Access Rights** tab, you will find a **Technical Features** checkbox. Let's check it and save.

Now we need to reload the page in our web browser. Then we should see in the **Settings** menu a new **Technical** menu section giving access to many Odoo server internals.

The **Technical** menu option allows us to inspect and edit all Odoo configurations stored in the database, from user interface to security and other system parameters. You will be learning more about many of these throughout the book.

Activating the Developer mode

The Developer mode enables a combobox near the top of Odoo windows, making a few advanced configuration options available throughout the application. It also disables the minification of JavaScript and CSS used by the web client, making it easier to debug client-side behavior.

To enable it, open the drop-down menu from the top-right corner of the browser window, next to the username, and select the **About Odoo** option. In the **About** dialog, click on the **Activate the developer mode** button at the top-right corner.

After this, we will see a **Debug View** combo box at the top left of the current form area.

Installing third-party modules

Making new modules available in an Odoo instance so they can be installed is something that newcomers to Odoo frequently find confusing. But it doesn't have to be so, so let's demystify it.

Finding community modules

There are many Odoo modules available from the Internet. The apps.odoo.com website is a catalogue of modules that can be downloaded and installed in your system. The **Odoo Community Association (OCA)** coordinates community contributions and maintains quite a few module repositories on GitHub, at https://github.com/OCA/

To add a module to an Odoo installation we could just copy it into the `addons` directory, alongside the official modules. In our case, the `addons` directory is at `~/odoo-dev/odoo/addons/`. This might not be the best option for us, since our Odoo installation is based on a version controlled code repository, and we will want to keep it synchronized with the GitHub repository.

Fortunately, we can use additional locations for modules, so we can keep our custom modules in a different directory, without having them mixed with the official addons.

As an example, we will download the OCA project `department` and make its modules available in our Odoo installation. This project is a set of very simple modules adding a Department field on several forms, such as Projects or CRM Opportunities.

To get the source code from GitHub:

```
$ cd ~/odoo-dev
$ git clone https://github.com/OCA/department.git -b 8.0
```

We used the optional `-b` option to make sure we are downloading the modules for the 8.0 version. Since at the moment of writing 8.0 is the projects default branch we could have omitted it.

After this, we will have a new `/department` directory alongside the `/odoo` directory, containing the modules. Now we need to let Odoo know about this new module directory.

Configuring the addons path

The Odoo server has a configuration option called `addons-path` setting where to look for modules. By default this points at the `/addons` directory where the Odoo server is running.

Fortunately, we can provide Odoo not only one, but a list of directories where modules can be found. This allows us to keep our custom modules in a different directory, without having them mixed with the official addons.

Let's start the server with an addons path including our new module directory:

```
$ cd ~/odoo-dev/odoo
$ ./odoo.py -d v8dev --addons-path="../department,./addons"
```

If you look closer at the server log you will notice a line reporting the addons path in use: **INFO ? openerp: addons paths:** (...). Confirm that it contains our `department` directory.

Updating the module list

We still need to ask Odoo to update its module list before these new modules are available to install.

For this we need the **Technical** menu enabled, since the **Update Modules List** menu option is provided by it. It can be found in the **Modules** section of the **Settings** menu.

After running the modules list update we can confirm the new modules are available to install. In the **Local Modules** list, remove the `Apps` filter and search for `department`. You should see the new modules available.

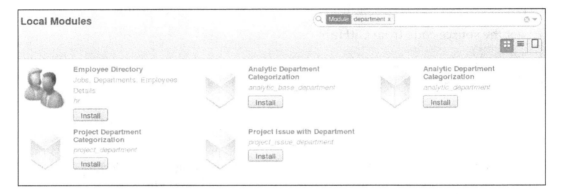

Summary

In this chapter, you learned how to set up a Debian system to host Odoo and to install it from GitHub sources. We also learned how to create Odoo databases and run Odoo instances. To allow developers to use their favorite tools in their personal workstation, we also explained how to configure file sharing in the Odoo host.

We should now have a functioning Odoo environment to work with and be comfortable managing databases and instances.

With this in place, we're ready to go straight into the action. In the next chapter we will create from scratch our first Odoo module and understand the main elements it involves.

So let's get started!

2
Building Your First Odoo Application

Developing in Odoo most of the time means creating our own modules. In this chapter, we will create our first Odoo application, and you will learn the steps needed make it available to Odoo and install it.

Inspired by the notable `todomvc.com` project, we will build a simple to-do application. It should allow us to add new tasks, then mark them as completed, and finally clear the task list of all completed tasks.

You will learn how Odoo follows an MVC architecture, and we will go through the following layers during the to-do application implementation:

- The **model**, defining the structure of the data
- The **view**, describing the user interface
- The **controller**, supporting the business logic of the application

The model layer is defined with Python objects that have their data is stored in the PostgreSQL database. The database mapping is automatically managed by Odoo, and the mechanism responsible for this is the **object relational model**, **(ORM)**.

The view layer describes the user interface. Views are defined using XML, which is used by the web client framework to generate data-aware HTML views.

The web client views perform data persistent actions by interacting with the server ORM. These can be basic operations such as write or delete, but can also invoke methods defined in the ORM Python objects, performing more complex business logic. This is what we refer to as the controller layer.

 Note that the concept of controller mentioned here is different from the Odoo web development controllers. Those are program endpoints that web pages can call to perform actions.

With this approach, you will be able to gradually learn about the basic building blocks that make up an application and experience the iterative process of building an Odoo module from scratch.

Understanding applications and modules

It's common to hear about Odoo modules and applications. But what exactly is the difference between them? **Modules** are building blocks of Odoo applications. A module can add or modify Odoo features. It is supported by a directory containing a manifest or descriptor file (named __openerp__.py) and the remaining files that implement its features. Sometimes, modules can also be referred to as "add-ons." **Applications** are not different from regular modules, but functionally, they provide a central feature, around which other modules add features or options. They provide the core elements for a functional area, such as accounting or HR, around which other modules add features. Because of this, they are highlighted in the Odoo **Apps** menu.

Modifying and extending modules

In the example that will follow, we will create a new module with as few dependencies as possible.

This will not be the typical case, however. The most frequent situation is where modifications or extensions are needed on an already existing module to fit some specific use cases.

The golden rule is that we shouldn't modify existing modules by changing them directly. It's considered bad practice to modify existing modules. This is especially true for the official modules provided by Odoo. Doing so does not allow a clear separation between the original module code and our modifications, and makes it difficult to apply upgrades.

Instead, we should create new modules to be applied on top of the modules we want to modify, and implement those changes. This is one of Odoo's main strengths: it provides "inheritance" mechanisms that allow custom modules to extend existing modules, either official or from the community. The inheritance is possible at all levels data models, business logic, and user interface layers.

Right now, we will create a completely new module, without extending any existing module, to focus on the different parts and steps involved in module creation. We will just take a brief look at each part, since each will be studied in more detail in the later chapters. Once we are comfortable with creating a new module, we can dive into the inheritance mechanisms, which will be introduced in the next chapter.

Creating a new module

Our module will be a very simple application to keep to-do tasks. These tasks will have a single text field, for the description, and a checkbox to mark them as complete. We will also have a button to clean the to-do list from the old completed tasks.

These are very simple specifications, but throughout the book we will gradually add new features to it, to make it more interesting for the users.

Enough talk, let's start coding and create our new module.

Following the instructions in *Chapter 1, Getting Started with Odoo Development*, we should have the Odoo server at /odoo-dev/odoo/. To keep things tidy, we will create a new directory alongside it to host our custom modules:

```
$ mkdir ~/odoo-dev/custom-addons
```

An Odoo module is a directory containing an __openerp__.py descriptor file. This is still a legacy from when Odoo was named OpenERP, and in the future is expected to become __odoo__.py.

It also needs to be Python importable, so it must also have an __init__.py file.

The module's directory name will be its technical name. We will use todo_app for it. The technical name must be a valid Python identifier: it should begin with a letter and can only contain letters, numbers, and the underscore character. The following commands create the module directory and create an empty __init__.py file in it:

```
$ mkdir ~/odoo-dev/custom-addons/todo_app
$ touch ~/odoo-dev/custom-addons/todo_app/__init__.py
```

Next we need to create the descriptor file. It should contain only a Python dictionary with about a dozen possible attributes, of which only the `name` attribute is required. A longer `description` attribute and the `author` also have some visibility and are advised.

We should now add an `__openerp__.py` file alongside the `__init__.py` file with the following content:

```
{
    'name': 'To-Do Application',
    'description': 'Manage your personal Tasks with this module.',
    'author': 'Daniel Reis',
    'depends': ['mail'],
    'application': True,
}
```

The `depends` attribute can have a list of other modules required. Odoo will have them automatically installed when this module is installed. It's not a mandatory attribute, but it's advised to always have it. If no particular dependencies are needed, we should depend on the special `base` module. You should be careful to ensure all dependencies are explicitly set here, otherwise the module may fail to install in a clean database (due to missing dependencies) or have loading errors, if the other needed modules are loaded afterwards. For our application, we want to depend on the **mail** module because that is the module that adds the **Messaging** top menu, and we will want to include our new menu options there.

To be concise, we chose to use very few descriptor keys, but in a real word scenario it is recommended to also use these additional keys, since they are relevant for the Odoo app store:

- `summary` is displayed as a subtitle for the module.
- `version`, by default, is 1.0. Should follow semantic versioning rules (see `semver.org` for details).
- `license` identifier, by default is AGPL-3.
- `website` is a URL to find more information about the module. This can help people to find more documentation or the issue tracker to file bugs and suggestions.
- `category` is the functional category of the module, which defaults to Uncategorized. The list of existing categories can be found in the security Groups form (`Settings | User | Groups` menu), in the **Application** field drop-down list.

These other descriptor keys are also available:

- `installable` is by default `True`, but can be set to `False` to disable a module.
- `auto_install` if this is set to `True` this module is automatically installed if all its dependencies are already installed. It is used for **glue** modules.

Since Odoo 8.0, instead of the `description` key we can use a `README.rst` or `README.md` file in the module's top directory.

Adding to the addons path

Now that we have a new module, even if minimal, we want to make it available in Odoo.

For that, we need to make sure the directory the module is in is part of the addons path. And then we need to update the Odoo module list.

Both operations have been explained in detail in the previous chapter, but we will follow here with a brief overview of what is needed.

We will position in our work directory and start the server with the appropriate addons path configuration:

```
$ cd ~/odoo-dev
$ odoo/odoo.py -d v8dev --addons-path="custom-addons,odoo/addons" --save
```

The `--save` option saves the options you used in a config file. This spares you from repeating them the next time you restart the server: just run `./odoo.py` and the last saved options will be used.

Look closely at the server log. It should have an **INFO ? openerp: addons paths:** (...) line, and it should include our `custom-addons` directory.

Remember to also include any other addons directories you might be using. For instance, if you followed the last chapter's instructions to install the department repository, you might want to include it and use the option:

```
--addons-path="custom-addons,department,odoo/addons"
```

Now let's ask Odoo to acknowledge the new module we just added.

For that, in the **Modules** section of the **Settings** menu, select the **Update Modules List** option. This will update the module list adding any modules added since the last update to the list. Remember that we need the Technical Features enabled for this option to be visible. That is done by selecting the **Technical Features** checkbox for our user.

Installing the new module

The **Local Modules** option shows us the list of available modules. By default it shows only **Apps** modules. Since we created an application module we don't need to remove that filter to see it. Type "todo" in the search and you should see our new module, ready to be installed.

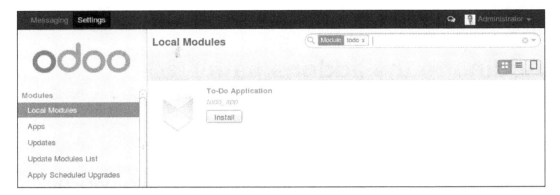

Now click on its **Install** button and you're done!

Upgrading a module

Developing a module is an iterative process, and you will want changes made on source files to be applied and visible in Odoo.

In most cases this is done by upgrading the module: look up the module in the **Local Modules** list and, since it is installed, you will see an **Upgrade** button available.

However, when the changes are only in Python code, the upgrade may not have an effect. Instead of a module upgrade, an application server restart is needed.

In some cases, if the module has changed both in data files and Python code, you might need both operations. This is a common source of confusion for newcomer Odoo developers.

But fortunately, there is a better way. The simplest and fastest way to make all our changes to a module effective is to stop (*Ctrl + C*) and restart the server process requesting our modules to be upgraded on our work database.

To start the server upgrading the todo_app module in the v8dev database, we will use:

```
$ ./odoo.py -d v8dev -u todo_app
```

The -u option (or --update in the long form) requires the -d option and accepts a comma-separated list of modules to update. For example, we could use: -u todo_app,mail.

Whenever you need to upgrade work in progress modules throughout the book, the safest way to do so is to go to the terminal window where you have Odoo running, stop the server, and restart it with the command above. Frequently pressing the Up arrow key will be enough, since it should bring you the previous command you used to start the server.

Unfortunately, updating the module list and uninstalling modules are both actions not available through the command line. These have to be done through the web interface, in the **Settings** menu.

Creating an application model

Now that Odoo knows about our new module, let's start by adding to it a simple model.

Models describe business objects, such as an opportunity, a sales order, or a partner (customer, supplier, and so on.). A model has a list of attributes and can also define its specific business.

Models are implemented using a Python class derived from an Odoo template class. They translate directly to database objects, and Odoo automatically takes care of that when installing or upgrading the module.

Some consider it good practice to keep the Python files for models inside a models subdirectory. For simplicity we won't be following that here, so let's create a todo_model.py file in the todo_app module main directory.

Add the following content to it:

```
# -*- coding: utf-8 -*-
from openerp import models, fields
class TodoTask(models.Model):
    _name = 'todo.task'
    name = fields.Char('Description', required=True)
    is_done = fields.Boolean('Done?')
    active = fields.Boolean('Active?', default=True)
```

The first line is a special marker telling the Python interpreter that this file has UTF-8, so that it can expect and handle non-ASCII characters. We won't be using any, but it's safer to use it anyway.

The second line makes available the models and fields objects from the Odoo core.

The third line declares our new model. It's a class derived from `models.Model`. The next line sets the `_name` attribute defining the identifier that will be used throughout Odoo to refer to this model. Note that the actual Python class name is meaningless to the other Odoo modules. The `_name` value is what will be used as an identifier.

Notice that this and the following lines are indented. If you're not familiar with Python you should know that this is important: indentation defines a nested code block, so these four line should all be equally indented.

The last three lines define the model's fields. It's worth noting that `name` and `active` are names of special fields. By default Odoo will use the `name` field as the record's title when referencing it from other models. The `active` field is used to inactivate records, and by default only active records will be shown. We will use it to clear away completed tasks without actually deleting them from the database.

Right now, this file is not yet used by the module. We must tell Odoo to load it with the module in the `__init__.py` file. Let's edit it to add the following line:

```
from . import todo_model
```

That's it. For our changes to take effect the module has to be upgraded. Locate the **To-Do** application in the **Local Modules** and click on its **Upgrade** button.

Now we can inspect the newly created model in the **Technical** menu. Go to **Database Structure | Models** and search for the **todo.task** model on the list. Then click on it to see its definition:

If everything went right, this will let us confirm that the model and our fields were created. If you made changes and don't see them here, try a server restart, as described before, to force all of the Python code to be reloaded.

We can also see some additional fields we didn't declare. These are the five reserved fields Odoo automatically adds to any model. They are as follows:

- `id`: This is the unique identifier for each record in the particular model.

- `create_date` and `create_uid`: These tell us when the record was created and who created it, respectively.

- `write_date` and `write_uid`: These tell us when the record was last modified and who modified it, respectively.

Adding menu entries

Now that we have a model to store our data, let's make it available on the user interface.

All we need to do is to add a menu option to open the `To-do Task` model so that it can be used. This is done using an XML file. Just as in the case of models, some people consider it good practice to keep the view definitions inside a `views` subdirectory.

We will create a new `todo_view.xml` data file in the module's top directory, and it will declare a menu item and the action performed by it:

```xml
<?xml version="1.0"?>
<openerp>
  <data>

    <!-- Action to open To-do Task list -->
    <act_window id="action_todo_task"
      name="To-do Task"
      res_model="todo.task"
      view_mode="tree,form" />

    <!-- Menu item to open To-do Task list -->
    <menuitem id="menu_todo_task"
      name="To-Do Tasks"
      parent="mail.mail_feeds"
      sequence="20"
      action="action_todo_task" />

  </data>
</openerp>
```

The user interface, including menu options and actions, is stored in database tables. The XML file is a data file used to load those definitions into the database when the module is installed or upgraded. This is an Odoo data file, describing two records to add to Odoo:

- The `<act_window>` element defines a client-side Window Action to open the `todo.task` model defined in the Python file, with the `tree` and `form` views enabled, in that order.

- The `<menuitem>` defines a menu item under the **Messaging** menu (identified by `mail.mail_feeds`), calling the `action_todo_task` action, which was defined before. The `sequence` lets us set the order of the menu options.

Now we need to tell the module to use the new XML data file. That is done in the `__openerp__.py` file using the `data` attribute. It defines the list of files to be loaded by the module. Add this attribute to the descriptor's dictionary:

```
'data': ['todo_view.xml'],
```

Now we need to upgrade the module again for these changes to take effect. Go to the **Messaging** menu and you should see our new menu option available.

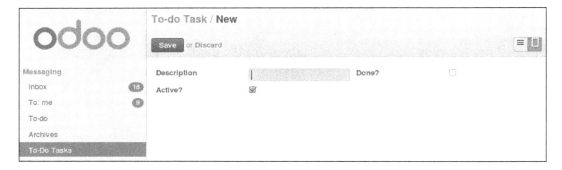

Clicking on it will open an automatically generated form for our model, allowing us to add and edit records.

Views should be defined for models to be exposed to the users, but Odoo is nice enough to do that automatically if we don't, so we can work with our model right away, without having any form or list views defined yet.

So far, so good! Let's improve our user interface now. Try the gradual improvements as shown in the next sections, doing frequent module upgrades, and don't be afraid to experiment.

In case an upgrade fails because of an XML error, don't panic! Comment out the last edited XML portions, or remove the XML file from __openerp__.py, and repeat the upgrade. The server should start correctly. Now read the error message in the server log carefully—it should point you to where the problem is.

Creating views – form, tree, and search

As we have seen, if no view is defined, Odoo will automatically generate basic views to get you going. But surely you would like to define the module views yourself, so that's what we'll do next.

Odoo supports several types of views, but the three main ones are: list (also called tree), form, and search views. We'll add an example of each to our module.

All views are stored in the database, in the ir.ui.view model. To add a view in a module, we declare a <record> element describing the view in an XML file that will be loaded into the database when the module is installed.

Creating a form view

Edit the XML we just created to add this <record> element just after the <data> opening tag at the top:

```
<record id="view_form_todo_task" model="ir.ui.view">
  <field name="name">To-do Task Form</field>
  <field name="model">todo.task</field>
  <field name="arch" type="xml">

    <form string="To-do Task">
      <field name="name"/>
      <field name="is_done"/>
      <field name="active" readonly="1"/>
    </form>

  </field>
</record>
```

This will add a record to the model ir.ui.view with the identifier view_form_todo_task. The view is for the model todo.task and named To-do Task Form. The name is just for information, does not have to be unique, but should allow one to easily identify what record it refers to.

The most important attribute is `arch`, containing the view definition. Here we say it's a form, and it contains three fields, and we chose to make the `active` field read only.

Formatting as a business document

The above provides a basic form view, but we can make some improvements to make it nicer. For `document` models Odoo has a presentation style that mimics a paper page. The form contains two elements: a `<header>`, containing action buttons, and a `<sheet>`, containing the data fields:

```
<form>
  <header>
  <!-- Buttons go here-->
  </header>
  <sheet>
      <!-- Content goes here: -->
      <field name="name"/>
      <field name="is_done"/>
  </sheet>
</form>
```

Adding action buttons

Forms can have buttons to run actions. These are able to trigger workflow actions, run Window Actions, such as opening another form, or run Python functions defined in the model.

They can be placed anywhere inside a form, but for document-style forms, the recommended place for them is the `<header>` section.

For our application, we will add two buttons to run methods of the `todo.task` model:

```
<header>
  <button name="do_toggle_done" type="object"
    string="Toggle Done" class="oe_highlight" />
  <button name="do_clear_done" type="object"
    string="Clear All Done" />
</header>
```

The basic attributes for a button are: `string` with the text to display on the button, the `type` of action it performs, and the `name` that is the identifier for that action. The optional `class` attribute can apply CSS styles, just like in regular HTML.

Organizing forms using groups

The `<group>` tag allows organizing the form content. Placing `<group>` elements inside a `<group>` element creates a two column layout inside the outer group. Group elements are advised to have a `name` to make it easier for other modules to extend on them.

We will use this to better organize our content. Let's change the `<sheet>` content of our form to match this:

```
<sheet>
  <group name="group_top">
    <group name="group_left">
      <field name="name"/>
    </group>
    <group name="group_right">
      <field name="is_done"/>
      <field name="active" readonly="1"/>
    </group>
  </group>
</sheet>
```

The complete form view

At this point, our record in `todo_view.xml` for the `todo.task` form view should look like this:

```
<record id="view_form_todo_task" model="ir.ui.view">
   <field name="name">To-do Task Form</field>
   <field name="model">todo.task</field>
   <field name="arch" type="xml">

     <form>
       <header>
         <button name="do_toggle_done" type="object"
                 string="Toggle Done" class="oe_highlight" />
         <button name="do_clear_done" type="object"
                 string="Clear All Done" />
       </header>
       <sheet>
           <group name="group_top">
           <group name="group_left">
             <field name="name"/>
           </group>
           <group name="group_right">
             <field name="is_done"/>
```

```
                <field name="active" readonly="1" />
            </group>
          </group>
        </sheet>
      </form>

    </field>
  </record>
```

Remember that for the changes to be loaded into our Odoo database, a module upgrade is needed. To see the changes in the web client, the form needs to be reloaded: either click again on the menu option that opens it, or reload the browser page (*F5* in most browsers).

Now, let's add the business logic for the actions buttons.

Adding list and search views

When viewing a model in list mode, a `<tree>` view is used. Tree views are capable of displaying lines organized in hierarchies, but most of the time they are used to display plain lists.

We can add the following tree view definition to `todo_view.xml`:

```
<record id="view_tree_todo_task" model="ir.ui.view">
  <field name="name">To-do Task Tree</field>
  <field name="model">todo.task</field>
  <field name="arch" type="xml">
    <tree colors="gray:is_done==True">
      <field name="name"/>
      <field name="is_done"/>
    </tree>
  </field>
</record>
```

We have defined a list with only two columns, `name` and `is_done`. We also added a nice touch: the lines for done tasks (`is_done==True`) are shown in grey.

At the top right of the list Odoo displays a search box. The default fields it searches for and available predefined filters can be defined by a `<search>` view.

As before, we will add this to the `todo_view.xml`:

```xml
<record id="view_filter_todo_task" model="ir.ui.view">
  <field name="name">To-do Task Filter</field>
  <field name="model">todo.task</field>
  <field name="arch" type="xml">
    <search>
      <field name="name"/>
      <filter string="Not Done"
              domain="[('is_done','=',False)]"/>
      <filter string="Done"
              domain="[('is_done','!=',False)]"/>
    </search>
  </field>
</record>
```

The `<field>` elements define fields that are also searched when typing in the search box. The `<filter>` elements add predefined filter conditions, using `domain` syntax that can be selected with a user click.

Adding business logic

Now we will add some logic to our buttons. Edit the `todo_model.py` Python file to add to the class the methods called by the buttons.

We will use the new API introduced in Odoo 8.0. For backward compatibility, by default Odoo expects the old API, and to create methods using the new API we need to use Python decorators on them. First we need to import the new API, so add it to the import statement at the top of the Python file:

```
from openerp import models, fields, api
```

The **Toggle Done** button's action will be very simple: just toggle the **Is Done?** flag. For logic on a record, the simplest approach is to use the `@api.one` decorator. Here `self` will represent one record. If the action was called for a set of records, the API would handle that and trigger this method for each of the records.

Inside the `TodoTask` class add:

```python
@api.one
def do_toggle_done(self):
    self.is_done = not self.is_done
    return True
```

As you can see, it simply modifies the `is_done` field, inverting its value. Methods, then, can be called from the client side and must always return something. If they return `None`, client calls using the XMLRPC protocol won't work. If we have nothing to return, the common practice is to just return the `True` value.

After this, if we restart the Odoo server to reload the Python file, the **Toggle Done** button should now work.

For the **Clear All Done** button we want to go a little further. It should look for all active records that are done, and make them inactive. Form buttons are supposed to act only on the selected record, but to keep things simple we will do some cheating, and it will also act on records other than the current one:

```
@api.multi
def do_clear_done(self):
    done_recs = self.search([('is_done', '=', True)])
    done_recs.write({'active': False})
    return True
```

On methods decorated with `@api.multi` the `self` represents a recordset. It can contain a single record, when used from a `form`, or several records, when used from a `list` view. We will ignore the `self` recordset and build our own `done_recs` recordset containing all the tasks that are marked as done. Then we set the `active` flag to `False`, in all of them.

The `search` is an API method returning the records meeting some conditions. These conditions are written in a domain, that is a list of triplets. We'll explore domains in more detail later.

The `write` method sets values at once on all elements of the recordset. The values to write are described using a dictionary. Using `write` here is more efficient than iterating through the recordset to assign the value to them one by one.

Note that `@api.one` is not the most efficient for these actions, since it will run for each selected record. The `@api.multi` ensures that our code runs only once even if there is more than one record selected when running the action. This could happen if an option for it were to be added on the list view.

Setting up access control security

You might have noticed, upon loading our module is getting a warning message in the server log: **The model todo.task has no access rules, consider adding one.**

The message is pretty clear: our new model has no access rules, so it can't be used by anyone other than the `admin` super user. As a super user the `admin` ignores data access rules, that's why we were able to use the form without errors. But we must fix this before other users can use it.

To get a picture of what information is needed to add access rules to a model, use the web client and go to: **Settings | Technical | Security | Access Controls List**.

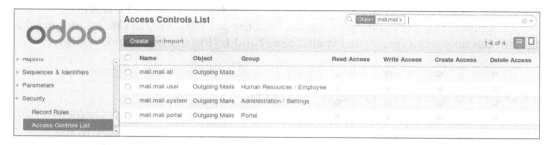

Here we can see the ACL for the `mail.mail` model. It indicates, per group, what actions are allowed on records.

This information needs to be provided by the module, using a data file to load the lines into the `ir.model.access` model. We will add full access on the model to the employee group. Employee is the basic access group nearly everyone belongs to.

This is usually done using a CSV file named `security/ir.model.access.csv`. Models have automatically generated identifiers: for `todo.task` the identifier is `model_todo_task`. Groups also have identifiers set by the modules creating them. The employee group is created by the base module and has identifier `base.group_user`. The line's name is only informative and it's best if it's kept unique. Core modules usually use a dot-separated string with the model name and the group. Following this convention we would use `todo.task.user`.

Now we have everything we need to know, let's add the new file with the following content:

```
id,name,model_id:id,group_id:id,perm_read,perm_write,perm_create,perm_
unlink
access_todo_task_group_user,todo.task.user,model_todo_task,base.group_
user,1,1,1,1
```

We must not forget to add the reference to this new file in the `__openerp__.py` descriptor's `data` attribute, so that should look like this:

```
'data': [
    'todo_view.xml',
    'security/ir.model.access.csv',
],
```

As before, upgrade the module for these additions to take effect. The warning message should be gone, and you can confirm the permissions are **OK** by logging in with the user `demo` (password is also `demo`) and trying the to-do tasks feature.

Row-level access rules

Odoo is a multi-user system, and we would like the to-do tasks to be private to each user. Fortunately for us, Odoo also supports row-level access rules. In the **Technical** menu they can be found in the **Record Rules** option, alongside the **Access Control List**.

Record rules are defined in the `ir.rule` model. As usual, we need a distinctive name. We also need the model they operate on and the domain to force access restriction. The domain filter uses the same domain syntax mentioned before, and used across Odoo.

Finally, rules may be either global (the `global` field is set to `True`) or only for particular security groups. In our case, it could perfectly be a global rule, but to illustrate the most common case, we will make it a group-specific rule, applying only to the employees group.

We should create a `security/todo_access_rules.xml` file with this content:

```xml
<?xml version="1.0" encoding="utf-8"?>
<openerp>
  <data noupdate="1">
    <record id="todo_task_user_rule" model="ir.rule">
        <field name="name">ToDo Tasks only for owner</field>
        <field name="model_id" ref="model_todo_task"/>
        <field name="domain_force">[('create_uid','=',user.id)]
        </field>
        <field name="groups" eval="[(4,ref('base.group_user'))]"/>
    </record>
  </data>
</openerp>
```

Notice the `noupdate="1"` attribute. It means this data will not be updated in module upgrades. This will allow it to be customized later, since module upgrades won't destroy user-made changes. But beware that this will also be so while developing, so you might want to set `noupdate="0"` during development, until you're happy with the data file.

In the `groups` field, you will also find a special expression. It's a one-to-many relational field, and they have special syntax to operate with. In this case, the `(4, x)` tuple indicates to append x to the records, and x is a reference to the employees group, identified by `base.group_user`.

As before, we must add the file to `__openerp__.py` before it can be loaded to the module:

```
'data': [
    'todo_view.xml',
    'security/ir.model.access.csv',
    'security/todo_access_rules.xml',
],
```

Adding an icon to the module

Our module is looking good. Why not add an icon to it to make it look even better? For that we just need to add to the module a `static/description/icon.png` file with the icon to use.

The following commands add an icon copied form the core `Notes` module:

```
$ mkdir -p ~/odoo-dev/custom-addons/todo_app/static/description
```

```
$ cd ~/odoo-dev/custom-addons/todo_app/static/description
```

```
$ cp ../odoo/addons/note/static/description/icon.png ./
```

Now, if we update the module list, our module should be displayed with the new icon.

Summary

We created a new module from the start, covering the most frequently used elements in a module: models, the three base types of views (form, list, and search), business logic in model methods, and access security.

In the process, you got familiar with the module development process, which involves module upgrades and application server restarts to make the gradual changes effective in Odoo.

Always remember, when adding model fields, an upgrade is needed. When changing Python code, including the manifest file, a restart is needed. When changing XML or CSV files, an upgrade is needed; also when in doubt, do both: upgrade the modules and restart the server.

In the next chapter, you will learn about building modules that stack on existing ones to add features.

3
Inheritance – Extending Existing Applications

One of Odoo's most powerful features is the ability to add features without directly modifying the underlying objects.

This is achieved through inheritance mechanisms, functioning as modification layers on top of existing objects. These modifications can happen at all levels: models, views, and business logic. Instead of directly modifying an existing module, we create a new module to add the intended modifications.

Here, you will learn how to write your own extension modules, empowering you to leverage existing core or community applications. As a relevant example, you will learn how to add Odoo's social and messaging features to your own modules.

Adding sharing capability to the To-Do app

Our To-Do application now allows users to privately manage their own to-do tasks. Won't it be great to take the app to another level by adding collaboration and social networking features to it? We will be able to share tasks and discuss them with other people.

We will do this with a new module to extend the previously created To-Do app to add these new features. Here is what we expect to achieve by the end of this chapter:

Road map for the user sharing features

Here is our work plan for the feature extensions to be implemented:

- Add fields to the **Task** model, such as the user who owns the task
- Modify the business logic to operate only on the current user's tasks, instead of all tasks the user is able to see
- Add the necessary fields to the views
- Add social networking features: the message wall and the followers

We will start creating the basic skeleton for the module alongside the `todo_app` module. Following the installation example in *Chapter 1, Getting Started with Odoo Development* we are hosting our modules at `~/odoo-dev/custom-addons/`:

```
$ mkdir ~/odoo-dev/custom-addons/todo_user
$ touch ~/odoo-dev/custom-addons/todo_user/__init__.py
```

Now create the __openerp__.py, containing this code:

```
{   'name': 'Multiuser To-Do',
    'description': 'Extend the To-Do app to multiuser.',
    'author': 'Daniel Reis',
    'depends': ['todo_app'], }
```

We haven't done that, but including the summary and category keys can be important when publishing modules to the Odoo online app store.

Next, we can install it. It should be enough to update the **Modules List** from the **Settings** menu, find the new module in the **Local Modules** list and click on its **Install** button. For more detailed instructions on discovering and installing a module you can refer back to *Chapter 1, Getting Started with Odoo Development*.

Now, let's start adding the new features to it.

Extending the to-do task model

New models are defined through Python classes. Extending them is also done through Python classes, but using an Odoo specific mechanism.

To extend an existing model we use a Python class with a _inherit attribute. This identifies the model to be extended. The new class inherits all the features of the parent Odoo model, and we only need to declare the modifications that we wish to introduce.

In fact, Odoo models exist outside our particular module, in a central registry. This registry can also be referred to as the pool, and can be accessed from model methods using self.env[<model name>]. For example, to reference the res.partner model we would write self.env['res.partner'].

To modify an Odoo model we get a reference to its registry class and then perform in place changes on it. This means that these modifications will also be available everywhere else where the model is used.

In the module loading sequence, during a server start, modifications will only be visible to the modules loaded afterward. So, the loading sequence is important and we should make sure that the module dependencies are correctly set.

Adding fields to a model

We will extend the todo.task model to add a couple of fields to it: the user responsible for the task, and a deadline date.

Create a new `todo_task.py` file declaring a class extending the original model:

```
# -*- coding: utf-8 -*-
from openerp import models, fields, api
class TodoTask(models.Model):
    _inherit = 'todo.task'
    user_id = fields.Many2one('res.users', 'Responsible')
    date_deadline = fields.Date('Deadline')
```

The class name is local to this Python file, and in general is irrelevant for other modules. The `_inherit` class attribute is the key here: it tells Odoo that this class is inheriting from the `todo.task` model. Notice the `_name` attribute absent. It is not needed because it is already inherited from the parent model.

The next two lines are regular field declarations. The `user_id` represents a user from the Users model, `res.users`. It's a `Many2one` field, the equivalent to a foreign key in database jargon. The `date_deadline` is a simple date field. In *Chapter 5, Models – Structuring the Application Data* we will be explaining in more detail the types of fields available in Odoo.

We still need to add to the `__init__.py` file the import statement to include it in the module:

```
from . import todo_task
```

To have the new fields added to the model's supporting database table we need to perform a module upgrade. If everything goes as expected, you should see the new fields when inspecting the `todo.task` model, in the **Technical** menu, **Database Structure | Models** option.

Modifying existing fields

As you can see, adding new fields to an existing model is quite straightforward. Since Odoo 8, modifying attributes on already existing fields is also possible. It's done by adding a field with the same name, and setting values only for the attributes to be changed.

For example, to add a help tooltip to the `name` field, we could add this line to the `todo_task.py` described above:

```
name = fields.Char(help="What needs to be done?")
```

If we upgrade the module, go to a to-do task form, and pause the mouse pointer over the **Description** field, the above tooltip text will be displayed.

Modifying model's methods

Inheritance also works at the business logic level. Adding new methods is simple: just declare their functions inside the inheriting class.

To extend existing logic, the corresponding method can be overridden by declaring a method with the exact same name, and the new method will replace the previous one. But it can extend the code of the inherited class, by using Python's `super()` keyword to call the parent method.

It's best to avoid changing the method's function signature (that is, keep the same arguments) to be sure that the existing calls on it will keep working properly. In case you need to add additional parameters, make them optional (with a default value) keyword arguments.

The original `Clear All Done` action is not appropriate for our task-sharing module anymore, since it clears all tasks regardless of their user. We need to modify it so that it clears only the current user tasks.

For this, we will override the original method with a new version that first finds the list of completed tasks for the current user, and then inactivates them:

```python
@api.multi
def do_clear_done(self):
    domain = [('is_done', '=', True),
      '|', ('user_id', '=', self.env.uid),
      ('user_id', '=', False)]
    done_recs = self.search(domain)
    done_recs.write({'active': False})
return True
```

We first list the `done` records to act upon using the `search` method with a filter expression. The filter expression follows an Odoo specific syntax referred to as a `domain`.

The filter domain used is defined the first instruction: it is a list of conditions, where each condition is a tuple.

These conditions are implicitly joined with an AND operator (`'&'` in domain syntax). To add an OR operation a pipe (`'|'`) is used in place of a tuple, and it will affect the next two conditions. We will go into more details about domains in *Chapter 6, Views - Designing the User Interface*.

The domain used here filters all done tasks (`'is_done'`, `'='`, `True`) that either have the current user as responsible (`'user_id'`, `'='`, `self.env.uid`) or don't have a current user set (`'user_id'`, `'='`, `False`).

What we just did was to completely overwrite the parent method, replacing it with a new implementation.

But this is not what we usually want to do. Instead we should extend the existing logic to add some additional operations to it. Otherwise we could break already existing features. Existing logic is inserted in an overriding method using Python's super() command, to call the parent's version of the method.

Let's see an example of this: we could write a better version of do_toggle_done() that only performs its action on the Tasks assigned to our user:

```
@api.one
def do_toggle_done(self):
    if self.user_id != self.env.user:
        raise Exception('Only the responsible can do this!')
    else:
        return super(TodoTask, self).do_toggle_done()
```

These are the basic techniques for overriding and extending business logic defined in model classes. Next we will see how to extend the user interface views.

Extending views

Forms, lists, and search views are defined using the arch XML structures. To extend views we need a way to modify this XML. This means locating XML elements and then introducing modifications on those points.

Inherited views allow just that. An inherited view looks like this:

```
<record id="view_form_todo_task_inherited" model="ir.ui.view">
  <field name="name">Todo Task form - User extension</field>
  <field name="model">todo.task</field>
  <field name="inherit_id" ref="todo_app.view_form_todo_task"/>
  <field name="arch" type="xml">
      <!-- ...match and extend elements here! ... -->
  </field
</record>
```

The inherit_id field identifies the view to be extended, by referring to its external identifier using the special ref attribute. External identifiers will be discussed in more detail in *Chapter 4, Data Serialization and Module Data*.

The natural way to locate elements in XML is to use XPath expressions. For example, taking the form view defined in the previous chapter, the XPath expression to locate the `<field name="is_done">` element is: `//field[@name]='is_done'`. This expression finds a `field` element with a `name` attribute equal to `is_done`. You can find more information on XPath at: `https://docs.python.org/2/library/xml.etree.elementtree.html#xpath-support`.

Having name attributes on elements is important because it makes it a lot easier to select them for extension points. Once the extension point is located, it can be modified or have XML elements added near it.

As a practical example, to add the `date_deadline` field before the `is_done` field, we would write in the `arch`:

```
<xpath expr="//field[@name]='is_done'" position="before">
  <field name="date_deadline" />
</xpath>
```

Fortunately Odoo provides shortcut notation for this, so most of the time we can avoid the XPath syntax entirely. Instead of the `xpath` element above we can use the element type we want to locate and its distinctive attributes. The above could also be written as:

```
<field name="is_done" position="before">
  <field name="date_deadline" />
</field>
```

Adding new fields next to existing fields is done often, so the `<field>` tag is frequently used as the locator. But any other tag can be used: `<sheet>`, `<group>`, `<div>`, and so on. The `name` attribute is usually the best choice for matching elements, but sometimes, we may need to use `string` (the displayed label text) or the CSS `class` element.

The `position` attribute used with the locator element is optional, and can have the following values:

- `after`: This is added to the parent element, after the matched node.
- `before`: This is added to the parent element, before the matched node.
- `inside` (the default value): This is appended to the content of the matched node.
- `replace`: This replaces the matched node. If used with empty content, it deletes an element.
- `attributes`: This modifies the XML attributes of the matched element (there are more details described following this list).

The `attributes` position allows us to modify the matched element's attributes. This is done using `<attribute name="attr-name">` elements with the new attribute values.

In the Task form, we have the **Active** field, but having it visible is not that useful. Maybe, we can hide it from the user. This can be done setting its `invisible` attribute:

```
<field name="active" position="attributes">
  <attribute name="invisible">1</attribute>
</field>
```

Setting the `invisible` attribute to hide an element is a good alternative to using the `replace` locator to remove nodes. Removing should be avoided, since it can break extension models that may depend on the deleted node.

Finally, we can put all of this together, add the new fields, and get the following complete inheritance view to extend the to-do tasks form:

```
<record id="view_form_todo_task_inherited" model="ir.ui.view">
  <field name="name">Todo Task form - User extension</field>
  <field name="model">todo.task</field>
  <field name="inherit_id" ref="todo_app.view_form_todo_task"/>
  <field name="arch" type="xml">
    <field name="name" position="after">
      <field name="user_id" />
    </field>
    <field name="is_done" position="before">
      <field name="date_deadline" />
    </field>
    <field name="name" position="attributes">
      <attribute name="string">I have to...</attribute>
    </field>
  </field
</record>
```

This should be added to a `todo_view.xml` file in our module, inside the `<openerp>` and `<data>` tags, as shown in the previous chapter.

 Inherited views can also be inherited, but since this creates more intricate dependencies, it should be avoided.

Also, we should not forget to add the `data` attribute to the `__openerp__.py` descriptor file:

```
'data': ['todo_view.xml'],
```

Extending tree and search views

Tree and search view extensions are also defined using the `arch` XML structure, and they can be extended in the same way as form views. We will follow example of a extending the list and search views.

For the list view, we want to add the user field to it:

```
<record id="view_tree_todo_task_inherited" model="ir.ui.view">
  <field name="name">Todo Task tree - User extension</field>
  <field name="model">todo.task</field>
  <field name="inherit_id" ref="todo_app.view_tree_todo_task"/>
  <field name="arch" type="xml">
    <field name="name" position="after">
      <field name="user_id" />
    </field>
  </field
</record>
```

For the search view, we will add search by user, and predefined filters for the user's own tasks and tasks not assigned to anyone:

```
<record id="view_filter_todo_task_inherited" model="ir.ui.view">
  <field name="name">Todo Task tree - User extension</field>
  <field name="model">todo.task</field>
  <field name="inherit_id" ref="todo_app.view_filter_todo_task"/>
  <field name="arch" type="xml">
    <field name="name" position="after">
      <field name="user_id" />
      <filter name="filter_my_tasks" string="My Tasks"
              domain="[('user_id','in',[uid,False])]" />
      <filter name="filter_not_assigned" string="Not Assigned"
              domain="[('user_id','=',False)]" />
    </field>
  </field>
</record>
```

Don't worry too much about the views-specific syntax. We'll cover that in more detail in *Chapter 6, Views - Designing the User Interface*.

More on using inheritance to extend models

We have seen the basic in place extension of models, which is also the most frequent use of inheritance. But inheritance using the _inherit attribute has more powerful capabilities, such as **mixin** classes.

We also have available the delegation inheritance method, using the _inherits attribute. It allows for a model to contain other models in a transparent way for the observer, while behind the scenes each model is handling its own data.

Let's explore these possibilities in more detail.

Copying features using prototype inheritance

The method we used before to extend a model used just the _inherit attribute. We defined a class inheriting the todo.task model, and added some features to it. The class attribute _name was not explicitly set; implicitly it was todo.task also.

But using the _name attribute allows us to create mixin classes, by setting it to the model we want to extend. Here is an example:

```
from openerp import models
class TodoTask(models.Model):
  _name = 'todo.task'
  _inherit = 'mail.thread'
```

This extends the todo.task model by copying to it the features of the mail.thread model. The mail.thread model implements the Odoo messages and followers features, and is reusable, so that it's easy to add those features to any model.

Copying means that the inherited methods and fields will also be available in the inheriting model. For fields this means that they will be also created and stored in the target model's database tables. The data records of the original (inherited) and the new (inheriting) models are kept unrelated. Only the definitions are shared.

These mixins are mostly used with abstract models, such as the mail.thread used in the example. Abstract models are just like regular models except that no database representation is created for them. They act like templates, describing fields and logic to be reused in regular models. The fields they define will only be created on those regular models inheriting from them. In a moment we will discuss in detail how to use this to add mail.thread and its social networking features to our module. In practice when using mixins we rarely inherit from regular models, because this causes duplication of the same data structures.

Odoo provides the delegation inheritance mechanism, which avoids data structure duplication, so it is usually preferred when inheriting from regular models. Let's look at it in more detail.

Embedding models using delegation inheritance

Delegation inheritance is the less frequently used model extension method, but it can provide very convenient solutions. It is used through the _inherits attribute (note the additional -s) with a dictionary mapping inherited models with fields linking to them.

A good example of this is the standard Users model, res.users, that has a Partner model embedded in it:

```
from openerp import models, fields
class User(models.Model):
    _name = 'res.users'
    _inherits = {'res.partner': 'partner_id'}
    partner_id = fields.Many2one('res.partner')
```

With delegation inheritance the model res.users embeds the inherited model res.partner, so that when a new User is created, a partner is also created and a reference to it is kept in the partner_id field of the User. It is similar to the polymorphism concept in object oriented programming.

All fields of the inherited model, Partner, are available as if they were User fields, through the delegation mechanism. For example, the partner name and address fields are exposed as User fields, but in fact they are being stored in the linked Partner model, and no data structure duplication occurs.

The advantage of this, compared to prototype inheritance, is that there is no need to repeat data structures in many tables, such as addresses. Any new model that needs to include an address can delegate that to an embedded Partner model. And if modifications are introduced in the partner address fields or validations, these are immediately available to all the models embedding it!

 Note that with delegation inheritance, fields are inherited, but methods are not.

Using inheritance to add social network features

The social network module (technical name `mail`) provides the message board found at the bottom of many forms, also called Open Chatter, the followers are featured along with the logic regarding messages and notifications. This is something we will often want to add to our models, so let's learn how to do it.

The social network messaging features are provided by the `mail.thread` model of the `mail` module. To add it to a custom model we need to:

- Have the module depend on `mail`.
- Have the class inherit from `mail.thread`.
- Have the Followers and Thread widgets added to the form view.
- Optionally, set up record rules for followers.

Let's follow this checklist:

Regarding #1, since our extension module depends on `todo_app`, which in turn depends on `mail`, the dependency on `mail` is already implicit, so no action is needed.

Regarding #2, the inheritance on `mail.thread` is done using the `_inherit` attribute we used before. But our to-do task extension class is already using the `_inherit` attribute. Fortunately it can also accept a list of models to inherit from, so we can use that to make it also include the inheritance on `mail.thread`:

```
_name = 'todo.task'
_inherit = ['todo.task', 'mail.thread']
```

The `mail.thread` model is an abstract model. Abstract models are just like regular models except that they don't have a database representation; no actual tables are created for them. Abstract models are not meant to be used directly. Instead they are expected to be used in mixin classes, as we just did. We can think of them as templates with ready-to-use features. To create an abstract class we just need it to use `models.AbstractModel` instead of `models.Model`.

For #3, we want to add the social network widgets at the bottom of the form. We can reuse the inherited view we already created, `view_form_todo_task_inherited`, and add this into its `arch` data:

```
<sheet position="after">
  <div class="oe_chatter">
    <field name="message_follower_ids" widget="mail_followers" />
    <field name="message_ids" widget="mail_thread" />
  </div>
</sheet>
```

The two fields we add here haven't been explicitly declared by us, but they are provided by the `mail.thread` model.

The final step is to set up record rules for followers. This is only needed if our model has record rules implemented that limit other users' access to its records. In this case, we need to make sure that the followers for each record have at least read access to it.

We do have record rules on the to-do task model so we need to address this, and that's what we will do in the next section.

Modifying data

Unlike views, regular data records don't have an XML `arch` structure and can't be extended using XPath expressions. But they can still be modified to replace values in their fields.

The `<record id="x" model="y">` element is actually performing an insert or update operation on the model: if x does not exist, it is created; otherwise, it is updated/written over.

Since records in other modules can be accessed using a `<model>.<identifier>` identifier, it's perfectly legal for our module to overwrite something that was written before by another module.

 Note that the dot is reserved to separate the module name from the object identifier, so they shouldn't be used in identifiers. Instead use the underscore.

As an example, let's change the menu option created by the todo_app module to into **My To Do**. For that we could add the following to the `todo_user/todo_view.xml` file:

```xml
<!-- Modify menu item -->
<record id="todo_app.menu_todo_task" model="ir.ui.menu">
    <field name="name">My To-Do</field>
</record>

<!-- Action to open To-Do Task list -->
<record model="ir.actions.act_window"
    id="todo_app.action_todo_task">
    <field name="context">
        {'search_default_filter_my_tasks': True}
    </field>
</record>
```

Extending the record rules

The To-Do application included a record rule to ensure that each task would only be visible to the user that created it. But now, with the addition of the social features, we need the task followers to also have access to them. The social network module does not handle this by itself.

Also, now tasks can have users assigned to them, so it makes more sense to have the access rules to work on the responsible user instead of the user who created the task.

The plan would be the same as we did for the menu item: overwrite the `todo_app.todo_task_user_rule` to modify the `domain_force` field to a new value.

Unfortunately this won't work this time. Remember the `<data no_update="1">` we used in the security rules XML file: it prevents later write operations on it.

Since updates on that record are being prevented, we need a workaround. That will be to delete that record and add a replacement for it in our module.

To keep things organized, we will create a `security/todo_access_rules.xml` file and add the following content to it:

```xml
<?xml version="1.0" encoding="utf-8"?>
<openerp>
  <data noupdate="1">

    <delete model="ir.rule" search="[('id', '=',
     ref('todo_app.todo_task_user_rule'))]" />

    <record id="todo_task_per_user_rule" model="ir.rule">
        <field name="name">ToDo Tasks only for owner</field>
        <field name="model_id" ref="model_todo_task"/>
        <field name="groups"
          eval="[(4, ref('base.group_user'))]"/>
        <field name="domain_force">
          ['|',('user_id','in', [user.id,False]),
             ('message_follower_ids','in',[user.partner_id.id])]
        </field>
    </record>

  </data>
</openerp>
```

This finds and deletes the `todo_task_user_rule` record rule from the `todo_app` module, and then creates a new `todo_task_per_user_rule` record rule. The domain filter we will now use makes a task visible to the responsible user `user_id`, to everyone if the responsible user is not set (equals `False`), and to all followers. The rule will run in a context where `user` is available and represents the current session user. The followers are partners, not User objects, so instead of `user.id`, we need to use `user.partner_id.id`.

 Working on data files with `<data noupdate="1">` is tricky because any later edit won't be updated on Odoo. To avoid that, temporarily use `<data noupdate="0">` during development, and change it back only when you're done with the module.

As usual, we must not forget to add the new file to the `__openerp__.py` descriptor file in the `data` attribute:

```
'data': ['todo_view.xml', 'security/todo_access_rules.xml'],
```

Notice that on module upgrade, the `<delete>` element will produce an ugly warning message, because the record to delete does not exist anymore. It is not an error and the upgrade will be successful, so we don't need to worry about it.

Summary

You should now be able to create new modules to extend existing modules. We saw how to extend the To-Do module created in the previous chapter.

New features were added onto the several layers that make up an application. We extended the Odoo model to add new fields, and extended the methods with its business logic. Next, we modified the views to make the new fields available on them. Finally, you learned how to extend a model by inheriting from other models, and we used that to add the social network features to our To-Do app.

With these three chapters, we had an overview of the common activities involved in Odoo development, from Odoo installation and setup to module creation and extension. The next chapters will focus on specific areas, most of which we visited briefly in these overviews. In the following chapter, we will address data serialization and the usage of XML and CSV files in more detail.

4
Data Serialization and Module Data

Most Odoo configurations, from user interfaces to security rules, are actually data records stored in internal Odoo tables. The XML and CSV files found in modules are not used to run Odoo applications. They are just a means to load those configurations into the database tables.

Because of this, an important part of Odoo modules is about representing (serializing) that data into files so that it can be later loaded into a database.

Modules can also have initial and demonstration (fixture) data. Data serialization allows adding that to our modules. Additionally, understanding Odoo data serialization formats is important in order to export and import data in the context of a project implementation.

Before we go into practical cases, we will first explore the external identifier concept, which is the key to Odoo data serialization.

Understanding external identifiers

All records in the Odoo database have a unique identifier, the id field.

It is a sequential number automatically assigned by the database. However, this automatic identifier can be a challenge when loading interrelated data: how can we reference a related record if we can't know beforehand what **database ID** will be assigned to it?

Odoo's answer to this is the external identifier. External identifiers solve this problem by assigning named identifiers to the data records to be loaded. A named identifier can be used by any other piece of record data to reference it later on. Odoo will take care of translating these identifier names into the actual database IDs assigned to them.

The mechanism behind this is quite simple: Odoo keeps a table with the mapping between the named External IDs and their corresponding numeric database IDs. That is the `ir.model.data` model.

To inspect the existing mappings, go to the **Technical** section of the **Settings** menu, and select the **Sequences & Identifiers | External Identifiers** menu item.

For example, if we visit the **External Identifiers** list and filter it by the `todo_app` module, we will see the external identifiers generated by the module created previously.

You can see that the external identifiers have a **Complete ID** label. This is composed of the module name and the identifier name joined by a dot, for example, `todo_app.action_todo_task`.

Since only the **Complete ID** is required to be unique, the module name ends up acting as a namespace for identifiers. This means that the same named identifier can be repeated in different modules, and we don't need to worry about identifiers in our module colliding with identifiers in other modules.

At the top of the list, you can see the `todo_app.action_todo_task` ID. This is the menu action we created for the module, which is also referenced in the corresponding menu item. By clicking on it, you can open a form with its details: the `action_todo_task` in the `todo_app` module maps to a specific record ID in the `ir.actions.act_window` model.

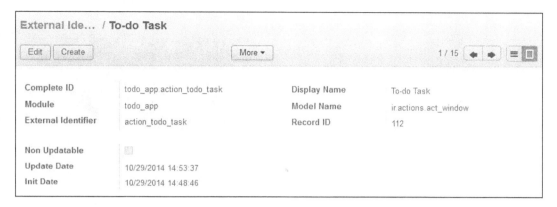

Besides providing a way for records to easily reference other records, External IDs also allow avoiding data duplication on repeated imports. If the External ID is already present, the existing record will be updated, instead of creating a new record. This is why, on subsequent module upgrades, previously loaded records are updated instead of being duplicated.

Finding External IDs

When preparing configuration and demonstration data files for modules, we frequently need to look up existing External IDs that are needed for references.

We can use the External Identifiers menu shown earlier, but the **Developer Menu** can provide a more convenient method for that. As you may recall from *Chapter 1, Getting Started with Odoo Development*, the **Developer Menu** is activated in the **About Odoo** option, and then, it is available at the top-left corner of the web client view.

To find the External ID for a data record, on the corresponding Form view, select the **View Metadata** option from the **Developer Menu**. This will display a dialog with the record's database ID and External ID (also known as XML ID).

As an example, to look up the Demo user ID, we can navigate to its **Form view** (**Settings | Users**) and select the **View Metadata** option, after which we will be shown this:

Metadata (res.users)	
ID:	4
XML ID:	base.user_demo
Creation User:	Administrator
Creation Date:	11/07/2014 08:10:59
Latest Modification by:	Administrator
Latest Modification Date:	11/07/2014 08:26:19

To find the External ID for view elements, such as form, tree, search, and action, the **Developer Menu** is also a good help. For that, use its **Manage Views** option or open the information for the desired view using the **Edit <view type>** options, and then select their **View Metadata** option.

Exporting and importing data

We will start exploring how data export and import work in Odoo, and from there, we will move on to the more technical details.

Exporting data

Data export is a standard feature available in any List view. To use it, we must first select the rows to export by selecting the corresponding checkboxes on the far left, and then select the **Export** option from the **More** button.

Here is an example, using the recently created to-do tasks:

The **Export** option takes us to a dialog form, where we can choose what to export. The **Import Compatible Export** option makes sure that the exported file can be imported back to Odoo. We will need to use this.

The export format can be CSV or Excel. We will prefer CSV file to get a better understanding of the export format. Next, we should pick the columns we want to export and click on the **Export To File** button. This will start the download of a file with the exported data.

If we follow these instructions and select the fields shown in the preceding screenshot, we should end up with a CSV text file similar to this:

```
"id","name","user_id/id","date_deadline","is_done"
"__export__.todo_task_1","Install Odoo","base.user_root","2015-01-
30","True"
"__export__.todo_task_2","Create dev database","base.user_
root","","False"
```

Notice that Odoo automatically exported an additional id column. This is an External ID that is automatically generated for each record. These generated External IDs use __export__ in place of an actual module name. New identifiers are only assigned to records that don't already have one, and from there on, they are kept bound to the same record. This means that subsequent exports will preserve the same External IDs.

Importing data

First we have to make sure the import feature is enabled. This is done in the **Settings** menu, **Configuration | General Settings** option. Under the **Import / Export** topic, make sure the **Allow users to import data from CSV files** checkbox is enabled.

With this option enabled, the List views show an **Import** option next to the **Create** button at the top of the list.

Let's perform a mass edit on our to-do data: open in a spreadsheet or a text editor the CSV file we just downloaded, then change a few values and add some new rows.

As mentioned before, the first id column provides a unique identifier for each row allowing already existing records to be updated instead of duplicated when we import the data back to Odoo. For new rows we may add to the CSV file, the id should be left blank, and a new record will be created for them.

After saving the changes on the CSV file, click on the **Import** option (next to the **Create** button) and we will be presented with the import assistant. There we should select the CSV file location on disk and click on **Validate** to check its format for correctness. Since the file to import is based on an Odoo export, there is a good chance it will be valid.

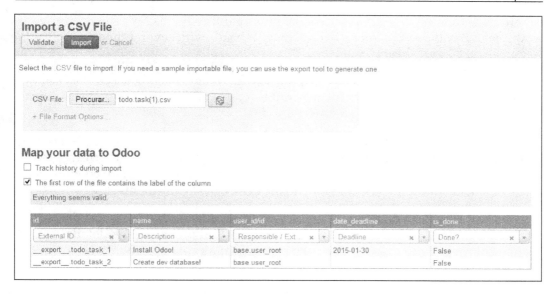

Now we can click on **Import** and there you go: our modifications and new records should have been loaded into Odoo.

Related records in CSV data files

In the example seen above, the user responsible for each task is a related record in the users model, with a **many to one** (or foreign key) relation. The column name used for it was `user_id/id` and the field values were External IDs for the related records, such as `base.user_root` for the administrator user.

Relation columns should have `/id` appended to their name, if using External IDs, or `/.id`, if using database (numeric) IDs. Alternatively, a colon (`:`) can be used in place of the slash for the same effect.

Similarly, **many to many** relations are also supported. An example of a many to many relations is the one between Users and Groups: each User can be in many Groups, and each Group can have many Users. The column name for this type of field should have appended a `/id`. The field values accept a comma-separated list of External IDs, surrounded by double quotes.

For example, the to-do task follower is a many-to-many relation between To-do Tasks and Partners. It's column name could be `follower_ids/id` and a field value with two followers could be:

```
"__export__.res_partner_1,__export__.res_partner_2"
```

Finally, **one to many** relations can also be imported through a CSV. The typical example of this type of relations is a document "head" with several "lines".

We can see an example for such a relation in the company model (form view available in the **Settings** menu): a company can have several bank accounts, each with its own details, and each bank account belongs to (has a many-to-one relation with) only one company.

It's possible to import companies along with their bank accounts in a single file. For this, some columns will correspond to the company, and other columns will correspond to the bank account details. The bank details column names should be prefixed with the one-to-many fields linking the company to the banks; bank_ids in this case.

The first bank account details goes in the same row as its related company data. The next bank account's details go in the next rows, but only the bank details related columns should have values; the company data columns should be empty in those lines.

Here is an example loading a company with three banks:

```
id,name,bank_ids/id,bank_ids/acc_number,bank_ids/state
base.main_company,YourCompany,__export__.res_partner_
bank_4,123456789,bank
,,__export__.res_partner_bank_5,135792468,bank
,,__export__.res_partner_bank_6,1122334455,bank
```

Notice that the two last lines begin with two commas: this corresponds to empty values in the first two columns, id and name, regarding the head company data. But the remaining columns, regarding bank accounts, have the values for the second and third bank records.

These are the essentials on working with export and import from the GUI. It's useful to set up data in new Odoo instances, or to prepare data files to be included in Odoo modules. Next we will learn more about using data files in modules.

Module data

Modules use data files to load their configurations into the database, initial data and demonstration data. This can be done using both CSV and XML files. For completeness, the YAML file format can also be used, but this is rarely used for data loading, so we won't be discussing it.

CSV files used by modules are exactly the same as those we have seen and used for the import feature. When using them in modules, the only additional restriction is that the file name must match the name of the model to which the data will be loaded.

A common example is security access, to load into the `ir.model.access` model. This is usually done using CSV files, and they should be named `ir.model.access.csv`.

Demonstration data

Odoo modules may install demo data. This is useful to provide usage examples for a module and data sets to be used in tests. It's considered good practice for modules to provide demonstration data. Demonstration data for a module is declared using the `demo` attribute of the `__openerp__.py` manifest file. Just like the `data` attribute, it is a list of file names with the corresponding relative paths inside the module.

We will be adding demonstration data to our `todo_user` module. We can start by exporting some data from the to-do tasks, as explained in the previous section. Next we should save that data in the `todo_user` directory with file name `todo.task.csv`. Since this data will be owned by our module, we should edit the `id` values to replace the `__export__` prefix in the identifiers with the module technical name.

As an example our `todo.task.csv` data file might look like this:

```
id,name,user_id/id,date_deadline
todo_task_a,"Install Odoo","base.user_root","2015-01-30"
todo_task_b","Create dev database","base.user_root",""
```

We must not forget to add this data file to the `__openerp__.py` manifest `demo` attribute:

```
'demo': ['todo.task.csv'],
```

Next time we update the module, as long as it was installed with demo data enabled, the content of the file will be imported. Note that this data will be rewritten whenever a module upgrade is performed.

XML files can also be used for demonstration data. Their file names are not required to match the model to load, because the XML format is much richer and that information is provided by the XML elements inside the file.

Let's learn more about what XML data files allow us to do that CSV files don't.

XML data files

While CSV files provide a simple and compact format to serialize data, XML files are more powerful and give more control over the loading process.

We have already used XML data files in the previous chapters. The user interface components, such as views and menu items, are in fact records stored in system models. The XML files in the modules are a means used to load those records into the server.

To showcase this, we will add a second data file to the todo_user module, named todo_data.xml, with the following content:

```xml
<?xml version="1.0"?>
<openerp>
  <data>
    <!-- Data to load -->
    <record model="todo.task" id="todo_task_c">
      <field name="name">Reinstall Odoo</field>
      <field name="user_id" ref="base.user_root" />
      <field name="date_deadline">2015-01-30</field>
    </record>
  </data>
</openerp>
```

This XML is equivalent to the CSV data file we have just seen in the previous section.

XML data files have a `<openerp>` element containing `<data>` elements, inside of which we can have have several `<record>` elements, corresponding to the CSV data rows.

A `<record>` element has two mandatory attributes, `model` and `id` (the external identifier for the record), and contains a `<field>` tag for each field to write on.

Note that the slash notation in field names is not available here: we can't use `<field name="user_id/id">`. Instead the `ref` special attribute is used to reference External IDs. We'll discuss the values for the relational "to many" fields in a moment.

The data noupdate attribute

When the data loading is repeated, existing records from the previous run are rewritten.

This is important to keep in mind: it means that upgrading a module will overwrite any manual changes that might have been made to the data. Notably, if views were modified with customizations, those changes will be lost with the next module upgrade. The correct procedure is to instead create inherited views for the changes we need, as discussed in the *Chapter 3, Inheritance – Extending Existing Applications*.

This overwrite behavior is the default, but it can be changed, so that when an already created record is loaded again no change is made to it. This is done by adding to the `<data>` element a `noupdate="1"` attribute. With this, its records will be created the first time they are loaded, and in subsequent module upgrades nothing will be done to them.

This allows for manually made customizations to be safe from module upgrades. It is often used with record access rules, allowing them to be adapted to implementation specific needs.

It is also possible to have more than one `<data>` section in the same XML file. We can take advantage of this to have a data set with `noupdate="1"` and another with `noupdate="0"`.

The `noupdate` flag is stored in the External Identifier information for each record. It's possible to edit it directly using the External Identifier form available in the Technical menu, with the **Non Updatable** checkbox.

 The `noupdate` attribute is tricky when developing modules, because changes made to the data later will be ignored, and Odoo won't pick up later modifications. A solution is to keep `noupdate="0"` during development and only set it to *1* once finished.

Defining Records in XML

Each `<record>` element has two basic attributes, `id` and `model`, and contains `<field>` elements assigning values to each column. As mentioned before, the `id` attribute corresponds to the record's External ID and the `model` to the target model where the record will be written. The `<field>` elements have available a few different ways to assign values. Let's look at them in detail.

Setting field values

The `<record>` element defines a data record, and contains `<field>` elements to set values on each field.

The `name` attribute of the field element identifies the field to be written.

The value to write is the element content: the text between the field's opening and closing tag. In general this is also suitable to set non-text values: for Booleans, `"0"`/`"1"` or `"False"`/`"True"` values will be correctly converted; for dates and datetimes, strings with `"YYYY-MM-DD"` and `"YYYY-MM-DD HH:MI:SS"` will be converted properly.

Setting values using expressions

A more advanced alternative to define a field value is using the `eval` attribute instead. This evaluates a Python expression and assigns the resulting value to the field.

The expression is evaluated in a context that, besides Python built-ins, also has some additional identifiers available. Let's have a look at them.

To handle dates, the following modules are available: `time`, `datetime`, `timedelta` and `relativedelta`. They allow calculating date values, something that is frequently used in demonstration (and test) data. For example, to set a value to yesterday we would use:

```
<field name="expiration_date"
    eval="(datetime.now() + timedelta(-1)).strftime('%Y-%m-%d')" />
```

Also available in the evaluation context is the `ref()` function, used to translate an External ID into the corresponding database ID. This can be used to set values for relational fields. As an example, we have used it before to set the value for the `user_id`:

```
<field name="user_id" eval="ref('base.group_user')" />
```

The evaluation context also has a reference available to the current Model being written through `obj`. It can be used together with `ref()` to access values from other records. Here is an example from the Sales module:

```
<value model="sale.order"
    eval="obj(ref('test_order_1')).amount_total" />
```

Setting values for relation fields

We have just seen how to set a value on a many-to-one relation field, such as `user_id`, using the `eval` attribute with a `ref()` function. But there is a simpler way.

The `<field>` element also has a `ref` attribute to set the value for a many-to-one field using an External ID. Using it, we can set the value for `user_id` using just:

```
<field name="user_id" ref="base.group_user" />
```

For one-to-many and many-to-many fields, a list of related IDs is expected, so a different syntax is needed, and Odoo provides a special syntax to write on this type of fields.

The following example, taken from the Fleet app, replaces the list of related records of a `tag_ids` field:

```
<field name="tag_ids"
  eval="[(6,0,
    [ref('vehicle_tag_leasing'),
    ref('fleet.vehicle_tag_compact'),
    ref('fleet.vehicle_tag_senior')]
)]" />
```

To write on a to many-field we use a list of triples. Each triple is a write command that does different things according to the code used:

- `(0,_ ,{'field': value})`: This creates a new record and links it to this one
- `(1,id,{'field': value})`: This updates values on an already linked record
- `(2,id,_)`: This unlinks and deletes a related record
- `(3,id,_)`: This unlinks but does not delete a related record
- `(4,id,_)`: This links an already existing record
- `(5,_,_)`: This unlinks but does not delete all linked records
- `(6,_, [ids])`: This replaces the list of linked records with the provided list

The underscore symbol used above represents irrelevant values, usually filled with 0 or `False`.

Shortcuts for frequently used Models

If we go back to *Chapter 2, Building Your First Odoo Application*, we can find in the XML files elements other than `<record>`, such as `<act_window>` and `<menuitem>`.

These are convenient shortcuts for frequently used Models that can also be loaded using regular `<record>` elements. They load data into base Models supporting the user interface and will be explored in more detail later, in *Chapter 6, Views - Designing the User Interface*.

For reference, so that we can better understand XML files we may encounter in existing modules, the following shortcut elements are available with the corresponding Models they load data into:

- `<act_window>`: This is the Window Actions model `ir.actions.act_window`
- `<menuitem>`: This is the Menu Items model `ir.ui.menu`
- `<report>`: This is the Report Actions model `ir.actions.report.xml`
- `<template>`: This is View QWeb Templates stored in model `ir.ui.view`
- `<url>`: This is the URL Actions model `ir.actions.act_url`

Other actions in XML data files

Until now we have seen how to add or update data using XML files. But XML files also allow performing other types of actions, sometimes needed to set up data. In particular, they are capable in deleting the data, execute arbitrary model methods, and trigger workflow events.

Deleting records

To delete a data record we use the `<delete>` element, providing it with either an `id` or a search domain to find the target record.

In *Chapter 3, Inheritance – Extending Existing Applications*, we had the need to remove a record rule added by the to-do app. In the `todo_user/security/todo_access_rules.xml` file a `<delete>` element was used, with a search domain to find the record to delete:

```
<delete
    model="ir.rule"
    search="[('id','=',ref('todo_app.todo_task_user_rule'))]"
/>
```

In this case the same exact effect could be achieved using the `id` attribute to identify the record to delete:

```
<delete model="ir.rule" id="todo_app.todo_task_user_rule" />
```

Triggering functions and workflows

An XML file can also execute methods during its load process through the `<function>` element. This can be used to set up demo and test data. For example, in the membership module it is used to create demonstration membership invoices:

```
<function
    model="res.partner"
    name="create_membership_invoice"
    eval="(ref('base.res_partner_2'),
        ref('membership_0'),
        {'amount':180})"
/>
```

This is calling the `create_membership_invoice()` method of the `res.partner` model. The arguments are passed as a tuple in the `eval` attribute. In this case we have a tuple with three arguments: the Partner ID, the Membership ID and a dictionary containing the invoice amount.

Another way XML data files can perform actions is by triggering Odoo workflows, through the `<workflow>` element.

Workflows can, for example, change the state of a sales order or convert it into an invoice. Here is an example taken from the `sale` module, converting a draft sales order to the confirmed state:

```
<workflow model="sale.order"
          ref="sale_order_4"
          action="order_confirm" />
```

The `model` is self-explanatory by now, and `ref` identifies the workflow instance we are acting upon. The `action` is the workflow signal sent to that workflow instance.

Summary

We have learned all the essentials about data serialization, and gained a better understanding of the XML aspects we saw in the previous chapters.

We also spent some time understanding External Identifiers, a central concept for data handling in general, and for module configurations in particular.

XML data files were explained in detail. We learned about the several options available to set values on fields and also to perform actions such as deleting records and calling model methods.

CSV files and the data import/export features were also explained. These are valuable tools for Odoo initial setup or for mass editing of data.

In the next chapter are will explore in detail how to build Odoo models and later learn more about building their user interfaces.

5
Models – Structuring the Application Data

In the previous chapters, we had an end-to-end overview of creating new modules for Odoo. In *Chapter 2*, *Building Your First Odoo Application*, a completely new application was built, and in *Chapter 3*, *Inheritance – Extending Existing Applications*, we explored inheritance and how to use it to create an extension module for our application. In *Chapter 4*, *Data Serialization and Module Data*, we discussed how to add initial and demonstration data to our modules.

In these overviews, we touched all the layers involved in building a backend application for Odoo. Now, in the following chapters, it's time to explain in more detail these several layers making up an application: models, views, and business logic.

In this chapter, you will learn how to design the data structures supporting an application, and how to represent the relations between them.

Organizing application features into modules

As before, we will use an example to help explain the concepts. One of the great things about Odoo is being able to pick any existing application or module and add, on top of it, those extra features you need. So we are going to continue improving our to-do modules, and in no time they will form a fully featured application!

It is a good practice to split Odoo applications into several smaller modules, each of them responsible for specific features. This reduces overall complexity and makes them easier to maintain and upgrade to later Odoo versions. The problem of having to install all these individual modules can be solved by providing an app module packaging all those features, through its dependencies. To illustrate this approach we will be implementing the additional features using new to-do modules.

Introducing the todo_ui module

In the previous chapter, we first created an app for personal to-dos, and then extended it so that the to-dos could be shared with other people.

Now we want to take our app to a new level by adding to it a kanban board and a few other nice user interface improvements. The kanban board will let us organize our tasks in columns, according to their stages, such as Waiting, Ready, Started or Done.

We will start by adding the data structures to enable that vision. We need to add stages and it will be nice if we add support for tags as well, allowing the tasks to be categorized by subject.

The first thing to figure out is how our data will be structured so that we can design the supporting Models. We already have the central entity: the to-do task. Each task will be in a stage, and tasks can also have one or more tags on them. This means we will need to add these two additional models, and they will have these relations:

- Each task has a stage, and there can be many tasks in each stage.
- Each task can have many tags, and each tag can be in many tasks.

This means that tasks have many to one relation with stages, and many to many relations with tags. On the other hand, the inverse relations are: stages have a one to many relationship with tasks and tags have a many to many relation with tasks.

We will start by creating the new `todo_ui` module and add the to-do stages and to-do tags models to it.

We've been using the `~/odoo-dev/custom-addons/` directory to host our modules. To create the new module alongside the existing ones, we can use these shell commands:

```
$ cd ~/odoo-dev/custom-addons
$ mkdir todo_ui
$ cd todo_ui
$ touch todo_model.py
$ echo "from . import todo_model" > __init__.py
```

Next, we should add the __openerp__.py manifest file with this content:

```
{   'name': 'User interface improvements to the To-Do app',
    'description': 'User friendly features.',
    'author': 'Daniel Reis',
    'depends': ['todo_app'] }
```

Note that we are depending on todo_app and not on todo_user. In general, it is a good idea to keep modules as independent as possible. When an upstream module is changed, it can impact all other modules that directly or indirectly depend on it. It's best if we can keep the number of dependencies low, and also avoid long dependency stacks, such as todo_ui → todo_user → todo_app in this case.

Now we can install the module in our Odoo work database and get started with the models.

Creating models

For the to-do tasks to have a kanban board, we need stages. Stages are the board columns, and each task will fit into one of these columns.

Let's add the following code to the todo_ui/todo_model.py file:

```
# -*- coding: utf-8 -*-
from openerp import models, fields, api

class Tag(models.Model):
    _name = 'todo.task.tag'
    name = fields.Char('Name', 40, translate=True)

class Stage(models.Model):
    _name = 'todo.task.stage'
    _order = 'sequence,name'
    _rec_name = 'name'  # the default
    _table = 'todo_task_stage'  # the default
    name = fields.Char('Name', 40, translate=True)
    sequence = fields.Integer('Sequence')
```

Here, we created the two new Models we will be referencing in the to-do tasks.

Focusing on the task stages, we have a Python class, Stage, based on the class models.Model, defining a new Odoo model, todo.task.stage. We also defined two fields, name and sequence. We can see some model attributes, (prefixed with an underscore) that are new to us. Let's have a closer look at them.

Model attributes

Model classes can have additional attributes used to control some of their behaviors:

- `_name`: This is the internal identifier for the Odoo model we are creating.

- `_order`: This sets the order to use when the model's records are browsed. It is a text string to be used as the SQL order by clause, so it can be anything you could use there.

- `_rec_name`: This indicates the field to use as the record description when referenced from related fields, such as a many to one relation. By default, it uses the name field, which is a commonly found field in models. But this attribute allows us to use any other field for that purpose.

- `_table`: This is the name of the database table supporting the model. Usually, it is left to be calculated automatically, and is the model name with the dots replaced by underscores. But it can be set to indicate a specific table name.

For completeness, we can also have the `_inherit` and `_inherits` attributes, as explained in *Chapter 3, Inheritance - Extending Existing Applications*.

Models and Python classes

Odoo models are represented by Python classes. In the preceding code, we have a Python class `Stage`, based on the `models.Model` class, used to define a new Odoo model `todo.task.stage`.

Odoo models are kept in a central registry, also referred to as `pool` in the previous versions. It is a dictionary keeping references of all the model classes available in the instance, and can be referenced by model name. Specifically, the code in a model method can use `self.env1['x']` or `self.env.get('x')` to get a reference to a class representing model x.

You can see that model names are important since they are the key used to access the registry. The convention for model names is to use a list of lowercase words joined with dots, like `todo.task.stage`. Other examples from the core modules are `project.project`, `project.task` or `project.task.type`. We should use the singular form: `todo.task` instead of `todo.tasks`. For historical reasons it's possible to find some core models not following this, such as `res.users`, but that is not the rule.

Model names must be globally unique. Because of this, the first word should correspond to the main application the module relates to. In our example, it is `todo`. Other examples from the core modules are `project, crm,` or `sale`.

Python classes, on the other hand, are local to the Python file where they are declared. The identifier used for them is only significant for the code in that file.

Because of this, class identifiers are not required to be prefixed by the main application they relate to. For example, there is no problem to call just `Stage` to our class for the `todo.task.stage` model. There is no risk of collision with possible classes with the same name on other modules.

Two different conventions for class identifiers can be used: `snake_case` or `CamelCase`. Historically, Odoo code used snake case, and it is still very frequent to find classes using that convention. But the recent trend is to use camel case, since it is the Python standard defined by the PEP8 coding conventions. You may have noticed that we are using the latter form.

Transient and Abstract models

In the preceding code, and in the vast majority of Odoo models, classes are based on the `models.Model` class. This type of models have database persistence: database tables are created for them and their records are stored until explicitly deleted.

But Odoo also provides two other model types to be used: Transient and Abstract models.

Transient models are based on the `models.TransientModel` class and are used for wizard-style user interaction. Their data is still stored in the database, but it is expected to be temporary. A vacuum job periodically clears old data from these tables.

Abstract models are based on the `models.AbstractModel` class and have no data storage attached to them. They act as reusable feature sets to be mixed in with other models. This is done using the Odoo inheritance capabilities.

Inspecting existing models

The information about models and fields created with Python classes is available through the user interface. In the **Settings** top menu, select the **Technical | Database Structure | Models** menu item. Here, you will find the list of all models available in the database. Clicking on a model in the list will open a form with its details.

This is a good tool to inspect the structure of a Model, since you have in one place the result of all additions that may come from several different modules. In this case, as you can see at the **In Modules** field, on the top right, the todo.task definitions are coming from the todo_app and todo_user modules.

In the lower area, we have some information tabs available: a quick reference for the model **Fields**, the **Access Rights** granted, and also list the **Views** available for this model.

We can find the model's **External Identifier**, by activating the **Developer Menu** and accessing its **View Metadata** option. These are automatically generated but fairly predictable: for the todo.task model, the **External Identifier** is model_todo_task.

The **Models** form is editable! It's possible to create and modify models, fields, and views from here. You can use this to build prototypes before carving them into proper modules.

Creating fields

After creating a new model, the next step is to add fields to it. Let's explore the several types of fields available in Odoo.

Basic field types

We now have a `Stage` model and will expand it to add some additional fields. We should edit the `todo_ui/todo_model.py` file, by removing some unnecessary attributes included before for the purpose of explanation, making it look like this:

```
class Stage(models.Model):
    _name = 'todo.task.stage'
    _order = 'sequence,name'
    # String fields:
    name = fields.Char('Name', 40)
    desc = fields.Text('Description')
    state = fields.Selection(
        [('draft','New'), ('open','Started'),('done','Closed')],
        'State')
    docs = fields.Html('Documentation')
    # Numeric fields:
    sequence = fields.Integer('Sequence')
    perc_complete = fields.Float('% Complete', (3, 2))
    # Date fields:
    date_effective = fields.Date('Effective Date')
    date_changed = fields.Datetime('Last Changed')
    # Other fields:
    fold = fields.Boolean('Folded?')
    image = fields.Binary('Image')
```

Here, we have a sample of the non-relational field types available in Odoo, with the basic arguments expected by each function. For most, the first argument is the field title, corresponding to the `string` keyword attribute. It's an optional argument, but it is recommended to be provided. If not, a title will be automatically generated from the field name.

There is a convention for date fields to use `date` as a prefix in their name. For example, we should use `date_effective` instead of `effective_date`. This can also apply to other fields, such as `amount_`, `price_` or `qty_`.

A few more arguments are available for most field types:

- `Char` accepts a second, optional argument, `size`, corresponding to the maximum text size. It's recommended to use it only if you have a good reason to.

- `Text` differs from `Char` in that it can hold multiline text content, but expects the same arguments.

- `Selection` is a drop-down selection list. The first argument is the list of selectable options and the second is the title string. The selection list items are (`'value'`, `'Title'`) tuples for the value stored in the database and the corresponding description string. When extending through inheritance, the `selection_add` argument can be used to append items to an existing selection list.

- `Html` is stored as a text field, but has specific handling to present HTML content on the user interface.

- `Integer` just expects a string argument for the field title.

- `Float` has a second optional argument, an (`x,y`) tuple with the field's precision: x is the total number of digits; of those, y are decimal digits.

- `Date` and `Datetime` data is stored in UTC time. There are automatic conversions made, based on the user time zone preferences, made available through the user session context. This is discussed in more detail in *Chapter 6, Views – Designing the User Interface*.

- `Boolean` only expects the field title to be set, even if it is optional.

- `Binary` also expects only a title argument.

Other than these, we also have the relational fields, which will be introduced later in this chapter. But now, there is still more to learn about these field types and their attributes.

Common field attributes

Fields also have a set of attributes we can use, and we'll explain these in more detail:

- `string` is the field title, used as its label in the UI. Most of the time it is not used as a keyword argument, since it can be set as a positional argument.

- `default` sets a default value for the field. It can be a static value or a callable, either a function reference or a lambda expression.

- `size` applies only to `Char` fields, and can set a maximum size allowed.

- `translate` applies to text fields, `Char`, `Text` and `Html`, and makes the field translatable: it can have different values for different languages.

- `help` provides the text for tooltips displayed to the users.
- `readonly=True` makes the field not editable on the user interface.
- `required=True` makes the field mandatory.
- `index=True` will create a database index on the field.
- `copy=False` has the field ignored when using the copy function. The non-relational fields are copyable by default.
- `groups` allows limiting the field's access and visibility to only some groups. It is a comma-separated list of strings for security group XML IDs.
- `states` expects a dictionary mapping values for UI attributes depending on values of the `state` field. For example: `states={'done':[('readonly',True)]}`. Attributes that can be used are `readonly`, `required`, and `invisible`.

For completeness, two other attributes are sometimes used when upgrading between Odoo major versions:

- `deprecated=True` logs a warning whenever the field is being used.
- `oldname='field'` is used when a field is renamed in a newer version, enabling the data in the old field to be automatically copied into the new field.

Reserved field names

A few field names are reserved to be used by the ORM:

- `id` is an automatic number uniquely identifying each record, and used as the database primary key. It's automatically added to every model.

The following fields are automatically created on new models, unless the `_log_access=False` model attribute is set:

- `create_uid` for the user that created the record
- `create_date` for the date and time when the record is created
- `write_uid` for the last user to modify the record
- `write_date` for the last date and time when the record was modified

This information is available from the web client, using the **Developer Mode** menu and selecting the **View Metadata** option.

There some built-in effects that expect specific field names. We should avoid using them for purposes other than the intended ones. Some of them are even reserved and can't be used for other purposes at all:

- `name` is used by default as the display name for the record. Usually it is a `Char`, but other field types are also allowed. It can be overridden by setting the `_rec_name` model attribute.

- `active` (type `Boolean`) allows inactivating records. Records with `active==False` will automatically be excluded from queries. To access them an `('active', '=', False)` condition must be added to the search domain, or `'active_test': False` should be added to the current context.

- `sequence` (type `Integer`) if present in a list view, allows to manually define the order of the records. To work properly it should also be in the model's `_order`.

- `state` (type `Selection`) represents basic states of the record's life cycle, and can be used by the state's field attribute to dynamically modify the view: some form fields can be made read only, required or invisible in specific record states.

- `parent_id`, `parent_left`, and `parent_right` have special meaning for parent/child hierarchical relations. We will shortly discuss them in detail.

So far we've discussed scalar value fields. But a good part of an application data structure is about describing the relationships between entities. Let's look at that now.

Relations between models

Looking again at our module design, we have these relations:

- Each task has a stage – that's a many to one relation, also known as a foreign key. The inverse relation is a one to many, meaning that each stage can have many tasks.

- Each task can have many tags – that's a many to many relation. The inverse relation, of course, is also a many to many, since each tag can also have many tasks.

Let's add the corresponding relation fields to the to-do tasks in our `todo_ui/todo_model.py` file:

```
class TodoTask(models.Model):
    _inherit = 'todo.task'
    stage_id = fields.Many2one('todo.task.stage', 'Stage')
    tag_ids = fields.Many2many('todo.task.tag', string='Tags')
```

The preceding code shows the basic syntax for these fields, setting the related model and the field's title string. The convention for relational field names is to append `_id` or `_ids` to the field names, for to one and to many relations, respectively.

As an exercise, you may try to also add on the related models, the corresponding inverse relations:

- The inverse of the Many2one relation is a One2many field on stages: each stage can have many tasks. We should add this field to the Stage class.

- The inverse of the Many2many relation is also a Many2many field on tags: each tag can also be used on many tasks.

Let's have a closer look at relational field definitions.

Many to one relations

Many2one accepts two positional arguments: the related model (corresponding to the comodel keyword argument) and the title string. It creates a field in the database table with a foreign key to the related table.

Some additional named arguments are also available to use with this type of field:

- ondelete defines what happens when the related record is deleted. Its default is set null, meaning it is set to an empty value if the related record is deleted. Other possible values are restrict, raising an error preventing the deletion, and cascade also deleting this record.

- context and domain are meaningful for the web client views. They can be set on the model to be used by default on any view where the field is used. They will be better explained in the *Chapter 6, Views - Designing the User Interface*.

- auto_join=True allows the ORM to use SQL joins when doing searches using this relation. By default this is False to be able to enforce security rules. If joins are used, the security rules will be bypassed, and the user could have access to related records the security rules wouldn't allow, but the SQL queries will be more efficient and run faster.

Many to many relations

The Many2many minimal form accepts one argument for the related model, and it is recommended to also provide the string argument with the field title.

At the database level, this does not add any column to the existing tables. Instead, it automatically creates a new relation table with only two ID fields with the foreign keys to the related tables. The relation table name and the field names are automatically generated. The relation table name is the two table names joined with an underscore with _rel appended to it.

These defaults can be manually overridden. One way to do it is to use the longer form for the field definition:

```
# TodoTask class: Task <-> Tag relation (long form):
tag_ids = fields.Many2many(
    'todo.task.tag',         # related model
    'todo_task_tag_rel',     # relation table name
    'task_id',               # field for "this" record
    'tag_id',                # field for "other" record
    string='Tasks')
```

Note that the additional arguments are optional. We could just set the name for the relation table and let the field names use the automatic defaults.

If you prefer, you may use the long form using keyword arguments instead:

```
# TodoTask class: Task <-> Tag relation (long form):
tag_ids = fields.Many2many(
    comodel_name='todo.task.tag',   # related model
    relation='todo_task_tag_rel',   # relation table name
    column1='task_id',              # field for "this" record
    column2='tag_id',               # field for "other" record
    string='Tasks')
```

Like many to one fields, many to many fields also support the `domain` and `context` keyword attributes.

On some rare occasions we may have to use these long forms to override the automatic defaults, in particular, when the related models have long names or when we need a second many to many relation between the same models.

 PostgreSQL table names have a limit of 63 characters, and this can be a problem if the automatically generated relation table name exceeds that limit. That is a case where we should manually set the relational table name using the `relation` attribute.

The inverse of the `Many2many` relation is also a `Many2many` field. If we also add a `Many2many` field to the tags, Odoo infers that this many to many relation is the inverse of the one in the task model.

The inverse relation between tasks and tags can be implemented like this:

```
# class Tag(models.Model):
#    _name = 'todo.task.tag'
#    Tag class relation to Tasks:
```

```
task_ids = fields.Many2many(
    'todo.task',    # related model
    string='Tasks')
```

One to many inverse relations

The inverse of a `Many2one` can be added to the other end of the relation. This has no impact on the actual database structure, but allows us easily browse from the "one" side the "many" side records. A typical use case is the relation between a document header and its lines.

On our example, with a `One2many` inverse relation on stages, we could easily list all the tasks in that stage. To add this inverse relation to stages, add the code shown here:

```
# class Stage(models.Model):
#    _name = 'todo.task.stage'
#    Stage class relation with Tasks:
    tasks = fields.One2many(
        'todo.task',    # related model
        'stage_id',     # field for "this" on related model
        'Tasks in this stage')
```

The `One2many` accepts three positional arguments: the related model, the field name in that model referring this record, and the title string. The two first positional arguments correspond to the `comodel_name` and `inverse_name` keyword arguments.

The additional keyword parameters available are the same as for many to one: `context`, `domain`, `ondelete` (here acting on the "many" side of the relation), and `auto_join`.

Hierarchical relations

Parent-child relations can be represented using a `Many2one` relation to the same model, to let each record reference its parent. And the inverse `One2many` makes it easy for a parent to keep track of its children.

Odoo also provides improved support for these hierarchic data structures: faster browsing through tree siblings, and simpler search with the additional `child_of` operator in domain expressions.

To enable these features we need to set the `_parent_store` flag attribute and add the helper fields: `parent_left` and `parent_right`. Mind that this additional operation comes at storage and execution time penalties, so it's best used when you expect to read more frequently than write, such as a the case of a category tree.

Revisiting the tags model defined in the `todo_ui/todo_model.py` file, we should now edit it to look like this:

```python
class Tags(models.Model):
    _name = 'todo.task.tag'
    _parent_store = True
    # _parent_name = 'parent_id'
    name = fields.Char('Name')
    parent_id = fields.Many2one(
        'todo.task.tag', 'Parent Tag', ondelete='restrict')
    parent_left = fields.Integer('Parent Left', index=True)
    parent_right = fields.Integer('Parent Right', index=True)
```

Here, we have a basic model, with a `parent_id` field to reference the parent record, and the additional `_parent_store` attribute to add hierarchic search support. When doing this, the `parent_left` and `parent_right` fields also have to be added.

The field referring to the parent is expected to be named `parent_id`. But any other field name can be used by declaring it with the `_parent_name` attribute.

Also, it is often convenient to add a field with the direct children of the record:

```python
child_ids = fields.One2many(
    'todo.task.tag', 'parent_id', 'Child Tags')
```

Referencing fields using dynamic relations

So far, the relation fields we've seen can only reference one model. The `Reference` field type does not have this limitation and supports dynamic relations: the same field is able to refer to more than one model.

We can use it to add a To-do Task field, **Refers to**, that can either refer to a `User` or a `Partner`:

```python
# class TodoTask(models.Model):
    refers_to = fields.Reference(
        [('res.user', 'User'), ('res.partner', 'Partner')],
        'Refers to')
```

You can see that the field definition is similar to a `Selection` field, but here the selection list holds the models that can be used. On the user interface, the user will first pick a model from the list, and then pick a record from that model.

This can be taken to another level of flexibility: a **Referencable Models** configuration table exists to configure the models that can be used in `Reference` fields. It is available in the **Settings | Technical | Database Structure** menu. When creating such a field we can set it to use any model registered there, with the help of the `referencable_models()` function in the `openerp.addons.res.res_request` module. In Odoo version 8, it is still using the old-style API, so we need to wrap it to use with the new API:

```
from openerp.addons.base.res import res_request
def referencable_models(self):
    return res_request.referencable_models(
        self, self.env.cr, self.env.uid, context=self.env.context)
```

Using the preceding code, the revisited version of the `Refers to` field would look like this:

```
# class TodoTask(models.Model):
    refers_to = fields.Reference(
        referencable_models, 'Refers to')
```

Computed fields

Fields can have values calculated by a function, instead of simply reading a database stored value. A computed field is declared just like a regular field, but has an additional argument `compute` with the name of the function used to calculate it.

In most cases computed fields involve writing some business logic, so we will develop this topic more in *Chapter 7, ORM Application Logic - Supporting Business Processes*. We can still explain them here, but keeping the business logic side as simple as possible.

Let's work on an example: stages have a `fold` field. We will add to tasks a computed field with the **Folded?** flag for the corresponding stage.

We should edit the `TodoTask` model in the `todo_ui/todo_model.py` file to add the following:

```
# class TodoTask(models.Model):
    stage_fold = fields.Boolean(
        'Stage Folded?',
        compute='_compute_stage_fold')

    @api.one
    @api.depends('stage_id.fold')
    def _compute_stage_fold(self):
        self.stage_fold = self.stage_id.fold
```

The preceding code adds a new `stage_fold` field and the `_compute_stage_fold` method used to compute it. The function name was passed as a string, but it's also allowed to pass it as a callable reference (the function identifier with no quotes).

Since we are using the `@api.one` decorator, `self` will represent a single record. If we used `@api.multi` instead, it would represent a recordset and our code would need to handle the iteration over each record.

The `@api.depends` is necessary if the computation uses other fields: it tells the server when to recompute stored or cached values. It accepts one or more field names as arguments and dot-notation can be used to follow field relations.

The computation function is expected to assign a value to the field or fields to compute. If it doesn't, it will error. Since `self` is a record object, our computation is simply to get the **Folded?** field using `self.stage_id.fold`. The result is achieved by assigning that value (writing it) to the computed field, `self.stage_fold`.

We won't be working yet on the views for this module, but you can make a quick edit on the task form to confirm if the computed field is working as expected: using the **Developer Menu** pick the **Edit View** option and add the field directly in the form XML. Don't worry: it will be replaced by the clean module view on the next upgrade.

Search and write on computed fields

The computed field we just created can be read, but it can't be searched or written. This can be enabled by providing specialized functions for that. Along with the `compute` function, we can also set a `search` function, implementing the search logic, and the `inverse` function, implementing the write logic.

In order to do this, our computed field declaration becomes like this:

```
# class TodoTask(models.Model):
    stage_fold = fields.Boolean(
        string='Stage Folded?',
        compute='_compute_stage_fold',
        # store=False)  # the default
        search='_search_stage_fold',
        inverse='_write_stage_fold')
```

The supporting functions are:

```
    def _search_stage_fold(self, operator, value):
        return [('stage_id.fold', operator, value)]

    def _write_stage_fold(self):
        self.stage_id.fold = self.stage_fold
```

The search function is called whenever a (field, operator, value) condition on this field is found in a search domain expression. It receives the operator and value for the search and is expected to translate the original search element into an alternative domain search expression.

The inverse function performs the reverse logic of the calculation, to find the value to write on the source fields. In our example, it's just writing on stage_id.fold.

Storing computed fields

Computed field's values can also be stored on the database, by setting store to True on their definition. They will be recomputed when any of their dependencies change. Since the values are now stored, they can be searched just like regular fields, so a search function is not needed.

Related fields

The computed field we implemented in the previous section is a special case that can be automatically handled by Odoo. The same effect can be achieved using Related fields. They make available, directly on a model, fields that belong to a related model, accessible using a dot-notation chain. This makes them usable in situations where dot-notation can't be used, such as UI forms.

To create a related field, we declare a field of the needed type, just like with regular computed fields, and instead of compute, use the related attribute indicating the dot-notation field chain to reach the desired field.

To-do tasks are organized in customizable stages and these is turn map into basic states. We will make them available on tasks, and will use this for some client-side logic in the next chapter.

Similarly to stage_fold, we will add a computed field on the task model, but now using the simpler Related field:

```
# class TodoTask(models.Model):
    stage_state = fields.Selection(
        related='stage_id.state',
        string='Stage State')
```

Behind the scenes, Related fields are just computed fields that conveniently implement search and inverse. This means that we can search and write on them out of the box, without having to write any additional code.

Model constraints

To enforce data integrity, models also support two types of constraints: SQL and Python.

SQL constraints are added to the table definition in the database and implemented by PostgreSQL. They are defined using the class attribute _sql_constraints. It is a list of tuples with the constraint identifier name, the SQL for the constraint, and the error message to use.

A common use case is to add unique constraints to models. Suppose we didn't want to allow the same user to have two active tasks with the same title:

```
# class TodoTask(models.Model):
    _sql_constraints = [
        ('todo_task_name_uniq',
         'UNIQUE (name, user_id, active)',
         'Task title must be unique!')]
```

Since we are using the user_id field added by the todo_user module, this dependency should be added to the depends key of the __openerp__.py manifest file.

Python constraints can use a piece of arbitrary code to check conditions. The checking function needs to be decorated with @api.constrains indicating the list of fields involved in the check. The validation is triggered when any of them is modified, and will raise an exception if the condition fails:

```
from openerp.exceptions import ValidationError
# class TodoTask(models.Model):
    @api.one
    @api.constrains('name')
    def _check_name_size(self):
        if len(self.name) < 5:
            raise ValidationError('Must have 5 chars!')
```

The preceding example prevents saving task titles with less than 5 characters.

Summary

We went through a thorough explanation of models and fields, using them to extend the To-do app with tags and stages on tasks. You learned how to define relations between models, including hierarchical parent/child relations. Finally, we saw simple examples of computed fields and constraints using Python code.

In the next chapter, we will work on the user interface for these back-end model features, making them available in the views used to interact with the application.

6
Views – Designing the User Interface

This chapter will help you build the graphical interface for your applications. There are several different types of views and widgets available. The concepts of context and domain also play an important role for an improved user experience, and you will learn more about them.

The `todo_ui` module has the model layer ready, and now it needs the view layer with the user interface. We will add new elements to the UI as well as modify existing views that were added in previous chapters.

The best way to modify existing views is to use inheritance, as explained in *Chapter 3, Inheritance – Extending Existing Applications*. However, for the sake of clarity, we will overwrite the existing views, replacing them with completely new views. This will make the topics easier to explain and follow.

A new XML data file for our UI needs to be added to the module, so we can start by editing the `__openerp__.py` manifest file. We will need to use some fields from the `todo_user` module, so it must be set as a dependency:

```
{    'name': 'User interface improvements to the To-Do app',
     'description': 'User friendly features.',
     'author': 'Daniel Reis',
     'depends': ['todo_user'],
     'data': ['todo_view.xml'] }
```

Let's get started with the menu items and window actions.

Window actions

Window actions give instructions to the client-side user interface. When a user clicks on a menu item or a button to open a form, it's the underlying action that instructs the user interface what to do.

We will start by creating the window action to be used on the menu items, to open the to-do tasks and stages views. Create the todo_view.xml data file with the following code:

```xml
<?xml version="1.0"?>
<openerp>
  <data>
    <act_window id="action_todo_stage"
        name="To-Do Task Stages"
        res_model="todo.task.stage"
        view_mode="tree,form" />

    <act_window id="todo_app.action_todo_task"
        name=" To-Do Tasks"
        res_model="todo.task"
        view_mode="tree,form,calendar,gantt,graph"
        target="current "
        context="{'default_user_id': uid}"
        domain="[]"
        limit="80" />

    <act_window id="action_todo_task_stage"
        name="To-Do Task Stages"
        res_model="todo.task.stage"
        src_model="todo.task"
        multi="False"/>
  </data>
</openerp>
```

Window actions are stored in the ir.actions.act_window model, and can be defined in XML files using the <act_window> shortcut that we just used.

The first action opens the task stages model, and uses only the basic attributes for a window action.

The second action uses an ID in the `todo_app` namespace to overwrite the original to-do task action of the `todo_app` module. It uses the most relevant window actions attributes:

- `name`: This is the title displayed on the views opened through this action.

- `res_model`: This is the identifier of the target model.

- `view_mode`: These are the view types to make available. The order is relevant and the first in the list is the view type opened by default.

- `target`: If this is set to `new`, it will open the view in a dialog window. By default, it is `current`, and opens the view in the main content area.

- `context`: This sets context information on the target views, which can be used to set default values on fields or activate filters, among other things. We will cover its details later in this chapter.

- `domain`: This is a domain expression setting a filter for the records that will be available in the opened views.

- `limit`: This is the number of records for each list view page, 80 by default.

The window action already includes the other view types that we will be exploring in this chapter: calendar, Gantt, and graph. Once these changes are installed, the corresponding buttons will be seen at the top-right corner, next to the list and form buttons. Notice that these won't work until we create the corresponding views.

The third window action demonstrates how to add an option under the **More** button, at the top of the view. These are the action attributes used to do so.

- `src_model`: This attribute indicates the model for which this window action should be made available in the **More** button.

- `multi`: This flag, if set to `True`, makes it available in the list view. Otherwise, it will be available in the form view.

Menu items

Menu items are stored in the `ir.ui.menu` model, and can be searched for in the **Settings** menu by navigating to **Technical | User Interface | Menu Items**. If we search for **Messaging**, we will see that it has **Organizer** as one of its submenus. With the help of the developer tools we can find the XML ID for that menu item: it is `mail.mail_my_stuff`.

We will replace the existing **To-do Task** menu item with a submenu that can be found by navigating to **Messaging | Organizer**. In the `todo_view.xml`, after the window actions, add this code:

```
<menuitem id="menu_todo_task_main"
  name="To-Do" parent="mail.mail_my_stuff" />
<menuitem id="todo_app.menu_todo_task"
  name="To-Do Tasks"
  parent="menu_todo_task_main"
  sequence="10"
  action="todo_app.action_todo_task" />
<menuitem id="menu_todo_task_stage"
  name="To-Do Stages"
  parent="menu_todo_task_main"
  sequence="20"
  action="action_todo_stage" />
```

The menu option data for the `ir.ui.menu` model can also be loaded using the `<menuitem>` shortcut element, as used in the preceding code.

The first menu item, **To-Do,** is a child of the `mail.mail_my_stuff` **Organizer** menu option. It has no action assigned, since it will be used as a parent for the next two options.

The second menu option rewrites the option defined in the `todo_app` module so that it is relocated under the **To-Do** main menu item.

The third menu item adds a new option to access the to-do stages. We will need it in order to add some data to be able to use stages in to-do tasks.

Context and domain

We have stumbled on context and domain several times. We have also seen that window actions are able to set values on them, and that relational fields can also use them in their attributes. Both concepts are useful to provide richer user interfaces. Let's see how.

Session context

The `context` is a dictionary carrying session data to be used by client-side views and by server processes. It can transport information from one view to another, or to the server-side logic. It is frequently used in window actions and relational fields to send information to the views opened through them.

Odoo sets some basic information about the current session on the context. The initial session information can look like this:

```
{'lang': 'en_US', 'tz': 'Europe/Brussels', 'uid': 1}
```

We have information on the current user ID and the language and time zone preferences for the user session.

When using an action on the client, such as clicking on a button, information about the currently selected records is added to the context:

- the `active_id` key is the ID of the selected record on a form,
- the `active_model` key is the model of the current record,
- the `active_ids` key is the list of IDs selected in the tree/list view.

The context can also be used to provide default values on fields or to enable filters on the target view. To set on the `user_id` field a default value corresponding to the session's current user we would use:

```
{'default_user_id': uid}
```

And if the target view has a filter named `filter_my_tasks`, we can enable it using:

```
{'search_default_filter_my_tasks': True}
```

Domain expressions

Domains are used to filter data records. Odoo parses them to produce the SQL WHERE expressions that are used to query the database.

When used on a window action to open a view, `domain` sets a filter on the records that will be available in that view. For example, to limit to only the current user's Tasks:

```
domain=[('user_id', '=', uid)]
```

The `uid` value used here is provided by the session context.

When used on a relation field, it will limit the selection options available for that field. The domain filter can also use values from other fields on the view. With this we can have different selection options available depending on what was selected on another field. For example, a contact person field can be made to show only the persons for the company that was selected on a previous field.

A domain is a list of conditions, where each condition is a (`'field'`, `'operator'`, `value`) tuple.

The left-hand field is where the filter will be applied to, and can use dot-notation on relation fields.

The operators that can be used are:

- The usual comparison operators: `<`, `>`, `<=`, `>=`, `=`, and `!=` are available.
- `=like` to match against the value pattern where the underscore symbol matches any single character, and `%` matches any sequence of characters.
- `like` for case-sensitive match against the `'%value%'` SQL pattern, and `ilike` for a case insensitive match. The `not like` and `not ilike` operators do the inverse operation.
- `child_of` finds the direct and indirect children, if parent/child relations are configured in the target model.
- `in` and `not in` check for inclusion in a list. In this case, the right-hand value should be a Python list. These are the only operators that can be used with list values. A curious special case is when the left-hand is a to-many field: here the `in` operator performs a contains operation.

The right-hand value can be a constant or a Python expression to be evaluated. What can be used in these expressions depends on the evaluation context available (not to be confused with the session context, discussed in the previous section). There are two possible evaluation contexts for domains: client side or server side.

For field domains and window actions, the evaluation is made client-side. The evaluation context here includes the fields available in the current view, and dot-notation is not available. The session context values, such as `uid` and `active_id`, can also be used. The `datetime` and `time` Python modules are available to use in date and time operations, and also a `context_today()` function returning the client current date.

Domains used in security record rules and in server Python code are evaluated on the server side. The evaluation context has the fields of the current record available, and dot-notation is allowed. Also available is the current session's `user` record. Using `user.id` here is the equivalent to using `uid` in the client side evaluation context.

The domain conditions can be combined using the logical operators: `'&'` for "AND" (the default), `'|'` for "OR", and `'!'` for "negation."

The negation is used before the condition to negate. For example, to find all tasks not belonging to the current user: `['!', ('user_id', '=', uid)]`

The "AND" and "OR" operate on the next two conditions. For example: to filter tasks for the current user or without a responsible user:

```
['|', ('user_id', '=', uid), ('user_id', '=', False)]
```

A more complex example, used in server-side record rules:

```
['|', ('message_follower_ids', 'in', [user.partner_id.id]),
    '|', ('user_id', '=', user.id),
        ('user_id', '=', False)]
```

This domain filters all records where the followers (a many to many relation field) contain the current user plus the result of the next condition. The next condition is again the union of two other conditions: the records where the user_id is the current session user or it is not set.

Form views

As we have seen in previous chapters, form views can follow a simple layout or a business document layout, similar to a paper document.

We will now see how to design business views and to use the elements and widgets available. Usually this would be done by inheriting the base view. But to make the code simpler, we will instead create a completely new view for to-do tasks that will override the previously defined one.

In fact, the same model can have several views of the same type. When an action asks to open a view type for a model, the one with the lowest priority is picked. Or as an alternative, the action can specify the exact identifier of the view to use. The action we defined at the beginning of this chapter does just that; the view_id tells the action to specifically use the form with ID view_form_todo_task_ui. This is the view we will create next.

Business views

In a business application we can differentiate auxiliary data from main business data. For example, in our app the main data is the to-do tasks, and the tags and stages are auxiliary tables used by it.

These business models can use improved business view layouts for a better user experience. If you recall the to-do task form view added in *Chapter 2*, *Building Your First Odoo Application*, it was already following the business view structure.

The corresponding form view should be added after the actions and menu items we added before, and its generic structure is this, use a lower priority of 10 (the default priority is 16):

```
<record id="view_form_todo_task_ui" model="ir.ui.view">
  <field name="name">view_form_todo_task_ui</field>
  <field name="model">todo.task</field>
```

```
<field name="arch" type="xml">
<field name="priority">10</field>
  <form>
    <header> <!-- Buttons and status widget --> </header>
    <sheet>  <!-- Form content --> </sheet>
    <!-- History and communication: -->
    <div class="oe_chatter">
      <field name="message_follower_ids"
             widget="mail_followers" />
      <field name="message_ids"
             widget="mail_thread" />
    </div>
  </form>

</field>
</record>
```

Business views are composed of three visual areas:

- A top header
- A sheet for the content
- A bottom history and communication section

The history and communication section, with the social network widgets at the lower end is added by inheriting our model from `mail.thread` (from the `mail` module), and adding at the end of the form view the elements in the XML sample as previously mentioned. We've also seen this in *Chapter 3, Inheritance - Extending Existing Applications*.

The header status bar

The status bar on top usually features the business flow pipeline and action buttons.

The action buttons are regular form buttons, and the most common next steps should be highlighted, using `class="oe_highlight"`. In `todo_ui/todo_view.xml` we can now expand the empty header to add a status bar to it:

```
<header>
  <field name="stage_state" invisible="True" />
  <button name="do_toggle_done" type="object"
          attrs="{'invisible':
                   [('stage_state','in',['done','cancel'])]}"
          string="Toggle Done" class="oe_highlight" />
  <!-- Add stage statusbar:  ... -->
</header>
```

Depending on where in the process the current document is, the action buttons available could differ. For example, a **Set as Done** button doesn't make sense if we are already in the "Done" state.

This can be done using the `states` attribute, listing the states where the button should be visible, like this: `states="draft,open"`.

For more flexibility we can use the `attrs` attribute, forming conditions where the button should be made invisible: `attrs="{'invisible': [('stage_state','in', ['done','cancel'])].`

These visibility features are also available for other view elements, and not only for buttons. We will be exploring that in more detail later in this chapter.

The business flow pipeline

The business flow pipeline is a status-bar widget on a field that represents the point in the flow where the record is. This is usually a **State** selection field, or a **Stage** many to one field. Both cases can be found across several Odoo modules.

The **Stage** is a many to one field using a model where the process steps are defined. Because of this they can be easily configured by end users to fit their specific business process, and are perfect to support kanban boards.

The **State** is a selection list featuring rather stable major steps in a process, such as **New, In Progress,** or **Done.** They are not configurable by end users but on the other hand are easier to use in business logic. States also have special support for views: the `state` attribute allows for an element to be selectively available to the user depending on the state of the record.

 It is possible to benefit from the best of both worlds, by using stages that are also mapped into states. This was what we did in the previous chapter, by making the **State** available in to-do task documents through a computed field.

To add a stage pipeline to our form header:

```
<!-- Add stage statusbar: ... -->
<field name="stage_id" widget="statusbar"
       clickable="True" options="{'fold_field': 'fold'}" />
```

The `clickable` attribute enables clicking on the widget, to change the document's stage or state. We may not want this if the progress through process steps should be done only through action buttons.

In the `options` attribute we can use some specific settings:

- `fold_field`, when using stages, is the name of the field that the stage model uses to indicate which stages should be shown folded.
- `statusbar_visible`, when using states, lists the states that should be always made visible, to keep hidden the other exception states used for less common cases. Example: `statusbar_visible="draft,open,done"`.

The sheet canvas is the area of the form containing the main form elements. It is designed to look like an actual paper document, and its data records are sometimes referred to as documents.

The document structure in general has these components:

- Title and subtitle information
- A smart button area, on the top right
- Document header fields
- A notebook with tab pages, with document lines or other details

Title and subtitle

When using the sheet layout, fields outside a `<group>` block won't have automatic labels displayed. It's up to the developer to control if and where to display the labels.

HTML tags can also be used to make the title shine. For best results, the document title should be in a `div` with the `oe_title` class:

```
<div class="oe_title">
  <label for="name" class="oe_edit_only"/>
  <h1><field name="name"/></h1>
  <h3>
    <span class="oe_read_only">By</span>
    <label for="user_id" class="oe_edit_only"/>
    <field name="user_id" class="oe_inline" />
  </h3>
</div>
```

Here we can see the use of regular HTML elements such as `div`, `span`, `h1` and `h3`.

Labels for fields

Outside `<group>` sections the field labels are not automatically displayed, but we can display them using the `<label>` element:

- The `for` attribute identify the field to get the label text from
- The `string` attribute to override the field's original label text

With the `class` attribute to we can also use CSS classes to control their presentation. Some useful classes are:

- `oe_edit_only` to display only when the form is in edit mode
- `oe_read_only` to display only when the form is in read mode

An interesting example is to replace the text with an icon:

```
<label for="name" string=" " class="fa fa-wrench" />
```

Odoo bundles the Font Awesome icons, being used here. The available icons can be browsed at `http://fontawesome.org`.

Smart buttons

The top right area can have an invisible box to place smart buttons. These work like regular buttons but can include statistical information. As an example we will add a button displaying the total number of to-dos for the owner of the current to-do.

First we need to add the corresponding computed field to `todo_ui/todo_model.py`. Add the following to the `TodoTask` class:

```
@api.one
def compute_user_todo_count(self):
    self.user_todo_count = self.search_count(
        [('user_id', '=', self.user_id.id)])

user_todo_count = fields.Integer(
    'User To-Do Count',
    compute='compute_user_todo_count')
```

Now we will add the button box with one button inside it. Right after the end of the `oe_title` div block, add the following:

```
<div name="buttons" class="oe_right oe_button_box">
    <button class="oe_stat_button"
            type="action" icon="fa-tasks"
            name="%(todo_app.action_todo_task)d"
            string=""
            context="{'search_default_user_id': user_id,
                    'default_user_id': user_id}"
            help="Other to-dos for this user" >

        <field string="To-dos" name="user_todo_count"
                widget="statinfo"/>
    </button>
</div>
```

The container for the buttons is a `div` with the `oe_button_box` class and also `oe_right`, to have it aligned to the right hand side of the form.

In the example the button displays the total number of to-do tasks the document responsible has. Clicking on it will browse them, and if creating new tasks the original responsible will be used as default.

The button attributes used are:

- `class="oe_stat_button"` is to use a rectangle style instead of a button.
- `icon` is the icon to use, chosen from the Font Awesome icon set.
- `type` will be usually `action`, for a window action, and `name` will be the ID of the action to execute. It can be inserted using the formula `%(action-external-id)d`, to translate the external ID into the actual ID number. This action is expected to open a view with related records.
- `string` can be used to add text to the button. It is not used here because the contained field already provides the text for it.
- `context` will set defaults on the target view, when clicking through the button, to filter data and set default values for new records created.
- `help` is the tooltip to display.

The button itself is a container and can have inside it's fields to display statistics. These are regular fields using the widget `statinfo`. The field should be a computed field, defined in the underlying module. We can also use static text instead or alongside the `statinfo` fields, such as: `<div>User's To-dos</div>`

Organizing content in a form

The main content of the form should be organized using `<group>` tags. A group is a grid with two columns. A field and its label take two columns, so adding fields inside a group will have them stacked vertically.

If we nest two `<group>` elements inside a top group, we will be able to get two columns of fields with labels, side by side.

```
<group name="group_top">
  <group name="group_left">
    <field name="date_deadline" />
    <separator string="Reference" />
    <field name="refers_to" />
  </group>
  <group name="group_right">
    <field name="tag_ids" widget="many2many_tags"/>
  </group>
</group>
```

Groups can have a `string` attribute, used as a title for the section. Inside a group section, titles can also be added using a `separator` element.

 Try the **Toggle Form Layout Outline** option of the **Developer** menu: it draws lines around each form section, allowing for a better understanding of how the current view is organized.

Tabbed notebooks

Another way to organize content is the notebook, containing multiple tabbed sections called pages. These can be used to keep less used data out of sight until needed or to organize a large number of fields by topic.

We won't need this on our to-do task form, but here is an example that could be added in the task stages form:

```
<notebook>
  <page string="Whiteboard" name="whiteboard">
    <field name="docs" />
  </page>
  <page name="second_page">
    <!-- Second page content -->
  </page>
</notebook>
```

It is good practice to have names on pages, to make it more reliable for other modules to extend them.

View elements

We have seen how to organize the content in a form, using elements such as `header`, `group`, and `notebook`. Now, we can take a closer look at the field and button elements, and what we can do with them.

Buttons

Buttons support these attributes:

- `icon` to display. Unlike smart buttons, icons available for regular buttons are those found in `addons/web/static/src/img/icons`.

- `string` is the button text description.

- `type` can be `workflow`, `object` or `action`, to either trigger a workflow signal, call a Python method, or run a window action.
- `name` is the workflow trigger, model method, or window action to run, depending on the button `type`.
- `args` can be used to pass additional parameters to the method, if the type is `object`.
- `context` sets values on the session context, which can have an effect after the windows action is run, or when a Python method is called. In the latter case, it can sometimes be used as an alternative to `args`.
- `confirm` adds a dialog with this message text asking for a confirmation.
- `special="cancel"` is used on wizards, to cancel and close the form. It should not be used with `type`.

Fields

Fields have these attributes available for them. Most are taken from what was defined in the model, but can be overridden in the view.

General attributes:

- `name`: identifies the field technical name.
- `string`: provides label text description to override the one provided by the model.
- `help`: tooltip text to use replace the one provided by the model.
- `placeholder`: provides suggestion text to display inside the field.
- `widget`: overrides the default widget used for the field's type. We will explore the available widgets a bit later in the chapter.
- `options`: holds additional options to be used by the widget.
- `class`: provides CSS classes to use for the field's HTML.
- `invisible="1"`: makes the field invisible.
- `nolabel="1"`: does not display the field's label, it is only meaningful for fields inside a `<group>` element.
- `readonly="1"`: makes the field non editable.
- `required="1"`: makes the field mandatory.

Attributes specific for some field types:

- `sum`, `avg`: for numeric fields, and in list/tree views, add a summary at the end with the total or the average of the values.
- `password="True"`: for text fields, displays the field as a password field.

- `filename`: for binary fields, is the field for the name of the file.

- `mode="tree"`: for One2many fields, is the view type to use to display the records. By default it is `tree`, but can also be `form`, `kanban` or `graph`.

For the Boolean attributes in general, we can use `True` or `1` to enable and `False` or `0` to disable them. For example, `readonly="1"` and `readonly="True"` are equivalent.

Relational fields

On relational fields, we can have some additional control on what the user is allowed to do. By default, the user can create new records from these fields (also known as quick create) and open the related record form. This can be disabled using the `options` field attribute:

```
options={'no_open': True, 'no_create': True}
```

The `context` and `domain` are also particularly useful on relational fields. The `context` can define default values for the related records, and the `domain` can limit the selectable records, for example, based on another field of the current record. Both `context` and `domain` can be defined in the model, but they are only used on the view.

Field widgets

Each field type is displayed in the form with the appropriate default widget. But other additional widgets are available and can be used as well:

Widgets for text fields:

- `email`: makes the e-mail text an actionable mail-to address.

- `url`: formats the text as a clickable URL.

- `html`: expects HTML content and renders it; in edit mode it uses a WYSIWYG editor to format the content without the need to know HTML.

Widgets for numeric fields:

- `handle`: specifically designed for sequence fields, this displays a handle to drag lines in a list view and manually reorder them.

- `float_time`: formats a float value as time in hours and minutes.

- `monetary`: displays a float field as a currency amount. The currency to use can be taken from a field, such as `options="{'currency_field': 'currency_id'}"`.

- `progressbar`: presents a float as a progress percentage, usually it is used on a computed field calculating a completion rate.

Some widgets for relational and selection fields:

- `many2many_tags`: displays a many to many field as a list of tags.
- `selection`: uses the Selection field widget for a many to one field.
- `radio`: allows picking a value for a selection field option using radio buttons.
- `kanban_state_selection`: shows a semaphore light for the kanban state selection list.
- `priority`: represents a selection as a list of clickable stars.

On-change events

Sometimes we need the value for a field to be automatically calculated when another field is changed. The mechanism for this is called on-change.

Since version 8, the on-change events are defined on the model layer, without the need for any specific markup on the views. This is done by creating the methods to perform the calculations and binding them to the triggering field(s) using a decorator `@api.onchange('field1', 'field2')`.

In previous versions, this binding was done in the view layer, using the `onchange` field attribute to set the class method called when that field was changed. This is still supported, but is deprecated. Be aware that the old-style on-change methods can't be extended using the new API. If you need to do that, you should use the old API.

Dynamic views

The elements visible as a form can also be changed dynamically, depending, for example, on the user's permissions or the process stage the document is in.

These two attributes allow us to control the visibility of user interface elements:

- `groups`: makes the element visible only for members of the specified security groups. It expects a comma separated list of group's XML IDs.
- `states`: makes the element visible only when the document is in the specified state. It expects a comma-separated list of State codes, and the document model must have a `state` field.

For more flexibility, we can instead set an element's visibility using client-side evaluated expressions. This is done using the `attrs` attribute with a dictionary mapping the `invisible` attribute to the result of a domain expression.

For example, to have the **refers_to** field visible in all states except `draft`:

```
<field name="refers_to"
       attrs="{'invisible': [('state','=','draft')]}" />
```

The `invisible` attribute is available in any element, not only fields. We can use it on notebook pages or groups, for example.

The `attrs` can also set values for two other attributes: `readonly` and `required`, but these only make sense for data fields, making them not editable or mandatory. With this we can add some client logic such as making a field mandatory, depending on the value from another field, or only from a certain state onward.

List views

Compared to form views, list views are much simpler. A list view can contain fields and buttons, and most of their attributes for forms are also valid here.

Here is an example of a list view for our To-do Tasks:

```xml
<record id="todo_app.view_tree_todo_task" model="ir.ui.view">
  <field name="name">To-do Task Tree</field>
  <field name="model">todo.task</field>
  <field name="arch" type="xml">
    <tree editable="bottom"
          colors="gray:is_done==True"
          fonts="italic: state!='open'" delete="false">
<field name="is_done" invisible="True"/>
<field name="stage_state" invisible="True"/>
      <field name="name"/>
      <field name="user_id"/>
    </tree>
  </field>
</record>
```

The attributes for the `tree` top element are:

- `editable`: makes the records editable directly on the list view. The possible values are `top` and `bottom`, the location where new records will be added.

- `colors`: dynamically sets the text color for the records, based on their content. It is a semicolon-separated list of `color:condition` values. The `color` is a CSS valid color (see `http://www.w3.org/TR/css3-color/#html4`), and the `condition` is a Python expression to evaluate on the context of the current record.

- `fonts`: dynamically modifies the font for the records based on their content. Similar to the `colors` attribute, but instead sets a font style to `bold`, `italic` or `underline`.

- `create`, `delete`, `edit`: if set to `false` (in lowercase), these disable the corresponding action on the list view.

Search views

The search options available on views are defined with a search view. It defines the fields to be searched when typing in the search box It also provides predefined filters that can be activated with a click, and data grouping options for the records on list and kanban views.

Here is a search view for the to-do tasks:

```
<record id="todo_app.view_filter_todo_task"
        model="ir.ui.view">
  <field name="name">To-do Task Filter</field>
  <field name="model">todo.task</field>
  <field name="arch" type="xml">
    <search>
      <field name="name" filter_domain="['|',
          ('name','ilike',self),('user_id','ilike',self)]"/>
      <field name="user_id"/>
      <filter name="filter_not_done" string="Not Done"
              domain="[('is_done','=',False)]"/>
      <filter name="filter_done" string="Done"
              domain="[('is_done','!=',False)]"/>
      <separator/>
      <filter name="group_user" string="By User"
              context="{'group_by': 'user_id'}"/>
    </search>
  </field>
</record>
```

We can see two fields to be searched for: `name` and `user_id`. On `name` we have a custom filter rule that makes the "if search" both on the description and on the responsible user. Then we have two predefined filters, filtering the not done and done tasks. These filters can be activated independently, and will be joined with an "OR" operator if both are enabled. Blocks of filters separated with a `<separator/>` element will be joined with an "AND" operator.

The third filter only sets a group-by context. This tells the view to group the records by that field, `user_id` in this case.

The `field` elements can use these attributes:

- `name`: identifies the field to use.

- `string`: provides a label text to use instead of the default.

- `operator`: allows us to use a different operator other than the default – "=" for numeric fields and `ilike` for the other field types.

- filter_domain: can be used to set a specific domain expression to use for the search, providing much more flexibility than the operator attribute. The text being searched for is referenced in the expression using self.

- groups: makes the search on the field available only for a list of security groups (identified by XML IDs).

For the filter elements these are the attributes available:

- name: is an identifier to use for inheritance or for enabling it through search_default_ keys in the context of window actions.

- string: provides label text to display for the filter (required).

- domain: provides the filter domain expression to be added to the active domain.

- context: is a context dictionary to add to the current context. Usually this sets a group_by key with the name of the field to group the records.

- groups: makes the search filter available only for a list of groups.

Other types of views

The most frequent view types used are the form and list views, discussed until now. Other than these, a few other view types are available, and we will give a brief overview on each of them. Kanban views won't be addressed now, since we will cover them in *Chapter 8, QWeb – Creating Kanban Views and Reports*.

Remember that the view types available are defined in the view_mode attribute of the corresponding window action.

Calendar views

As the name suggests, this view presents the records in a calendar. A calendar view for the to-do tasks could look like this:

```xml
<record id="view_calendar_todo_task" model="ir.ui.view">
  <field name="name">view_calendar_todo_task</field>
  <field name="model">todo.task</field>
  <field name="arch" type="xml">
    <calendar date_start="date_deadline" color="user_id"
              display="[name], Stage [stage_id]">
    <!-- Fields used for the text of display attribute -->
    <field name="name" />
    <field name="stage_id" />
    </calendar>
  </field>
</record>
```

The calendar attributes are these:

- `date_start`: This is the field for the start date (mandatory).
- `date_end`: This is the field for the end date (optional).
- `date_delay`: This is the field with the duration in days. This is to be used instead of `date_end`.
- `color`: This is the field used to color the calendar entries. Each value in the field will be assigned a color, and all its entries will have the same color.
- `display`: This is the text to be displayed in the calendar entries. Fields can be inserted using `[<field>]`. These fields must be declared inside the calendar element.

Gantt views

This view presents the data in a Gantt chart, which is useful for scheduling. The to-do tasks only have a date field for the deadline, but we can use it to have a basic Gantt view working:

```xml
<record id="view_gantt_todo_task" model="ir.ui.view">
  <field name="name">view_gantt_todo_task</field>
  <field name="model">todo.task</field>
  <field name="arch" type="xml">
    <gantt date_start="date_deadline"
           default_group_by="user_id" />
  </field>
</record>
```

Attributes that can be used for Gantt views are as follows:

- `date_start`: This is the field for the start date (mandatory).
- `date_stop`: This is the field for the end date. It can be replaced by the `date_delay`.
- `date_delay`: This is the field with the duration in days. It can be used instead of `date_stop`.
- `progress`: This is the field that provides completion percentage (between 0 and 100).
- `default_group_by`: This is the field used to group the Gantt tasks.

Graph views

The graph view type provides a data analysis of the data, in the form of a chart or an interactive pivot table.

We will add a pivot table to the to-do tasks. First, we need a field to be aggregated. In the `TodoTask` class, in the `todo_ui/todo_model.py` file, add this line:

```
effort_estimate = fields.Integer('Effort Estimate')
```

This should also be added to the to-do task form so that we can set some data on it. Now, let's add the graph view with a pivot table:

```xml
<record id="view_graph_todo_task" model="ir.ui.view">
  <field name="name">view_graph_todo_task</field>
  <field name="model">todo.task</field>
  <field name="arch" type="xml">
    <graph type="pivot">
      <field name="stage_id" type="col" />
      <field name="user_id" />
      <field name="date_deadline" interval="week" />
      <field name="effort_estimate" type="measure" />
    </graph>
  </field>
</record>
```

The `graph` element has a `type` attribute set to `pivot`. It can also be `bar` (default), `pie`, or `line`. In the case of `bar`, an additional `stacked="True"` can be used to make it a stacked bar chart.

The graph should contain fields that have these possible attributes:

- `name`: This identifies the field to use in the graph, as in other views.

- `type`: This describes how the field will be used, as a `row` group (default), as a `col` group (column), or as a `measure`.

- `interval`: only meaningful for date fields, this is the time interval used to group time data by `day`, `week`, `month`, `quarter` or `year`.

Summary

You learned more about Odoo views used to build the user interface. We started by adding menu options and the window actions used by them to open views. The concepts of context and domain were explained in more detail in following sections.

You also learned about designing list views and configuring search options using search views. Next, we had an overview of the other view types available: calendar, Gantt, and graph. Kanban views will be explored later, when you learn how to use QWeb.

We have already seen models and views. In the next chapter, you will learn how to implement server-side business logic.

7
ORM Application Logic – Supporting Business Processes

In this chapter, you will learn to write code to support business logic in your models and you will also learn how it can be activated on events and user actions. Using the Odoo programming API, we can write complex logic and wizards allow us to provide a rich user interaction with these programs.

To-do wizard

With the wizards, we can ask users to input information to be used in some processes. Suppose our to-do app users regularly need to set deadlines and the responsible persons for a large number of tasks. We could use an assistant to help them with this. It should allow them to pick the tasks to be updated and then choose the deadline date and/or the responsible user to set on them.

We will start by creating a new module for this feature: `todo_wizard`. Our module will have a Python file and an XML file, so the `todo_wizard/__openerp__.py` description will be as shown in the following code:

```
{ 'name': 'To-do Tasks Management Assistant',
  'description': 'Mass edit your To-Do backlog.',
  'author': 'Daniel Reis',
  'depends': ['todo_user'],
  'data': ['todo_wizard_view.xml'], }
```

The `todo_wizard/__init__.py` file to load our code is just one line, as follows:

```
from . import todo_wizard_model
```

Next, we need to describe the data model supporting our wizard.

Wizard model

A wizard displays a form view to the user, usually in a dialog window, with some fields to be filled in. These will then be used by the wizard logic.

This is implemented using the model/view architecture used for regular views, with a difference: the supporting model is based on `models.TransientModel` instead of `models.Model`.

This type of model is also stored in the database, but the data is expected to be useful only until the wizard is completed or canceled. Server vacuum processes regularly clean up old wizard data from the corresponding database tables.

The `todo_wizard/todo_wizard_model.py` file will define the three fields we need: the lists of tasks to update, the user responsible for them, and the deadline to set on them, as shown here:

```
# -*- coding: utf-8 -*-
from openerp import models, fields, api
from openerp import exceptions  # will be used in the code

import logging
_logger = logging.getLogger(__name__)

class TodoWizard(models.TransientModel):
    _name = 'todo.wizard'
    task_ids = fields.Many2many('todo.task', string='Tasks')
    new_deadline = fields.Date('Deadline to Set')
    new_user_id = fields.Many2one(
        'res.users',string='Responsible to Set')
```

It's worth noting that if we used a *one to many* relation, we would have to add the inverse *many to one* field on to-do tasks. We should avoid *many to one* relations between transient and regular models, and so we used a *many to many* relation that fulfills the same purpose without the need to modify the to-do task model.

We are also adding support to message logging. The logger is initialized with the two lines just before the `TodoWizard`, using the Python logging standard library. To write messages to the log we can use:

```
_logger.debug('A DEBUG message')
_logger.info('An INFO message')
_logger.warning('A WARNING message')
_logger.error('An ERROR message')
```

We will see some usage examples in this chapter.

Wizard form

The wizard form view looks exactly the same as regular forms, except for two specific elements:

- A `<footer>` section can be used to place the action buttons.
- A special `cancel` button type is available to interrupt the wizard without performing any action.

This is the content of our `todo_wizard/todo_wizard_view.xml` file:

```xml
<openerp>
  <data>
    <record id="To-do Task Wizard" model="ir.ui.view">
      <field name="name">To-do Task Wizard</field>
      <field name="model">todo.wizard</field>
      <field name="arch" type="xml">

        <form>
          <div class="oe_right">
            <button type="object" name="do_count_tasks"
                    string="Count" />
            <button type="object" name="do_populate_tasks"
                    string="Get All" />
          </div>
          <field name="task_ids" />
          <group>
            <group> <field name="new_user_id" /> </group>
            <group> <field name="new_deadline" /> </group>
          </group>
```

```
          <footer>
            <button type="object" name="do_mass_update"
                string="Mass Update" class="oe_highlight"
                attrs="{'invisible':
                        [('new_deadline','=',False),
                         ('new_user_id', '=',False)]}" />
            <button special="cancel" string="Cancel"/>
          </footer>
        </form>
      </field>
    </record>

    <!-- More button Action →
    <act_window id="todo_app.action_todo_wizard"
        name="To-Do Tasks Wizard"
        src_model="todo.task" res_model="todo.wizard"
        view_mode="form" target="new" multi="True" />
  </data>
</openerp>
```

The window action we see in the XML adds an option to the **More** button of the to-do task form by using the `src_model` attribute. `target="new"` makes it open as a dialog window.

You might also have noticed `attrs` in the **Mass Update** button used to make it invisible until either a new deadline or responsible user is selected.

This is how our wizard will look:

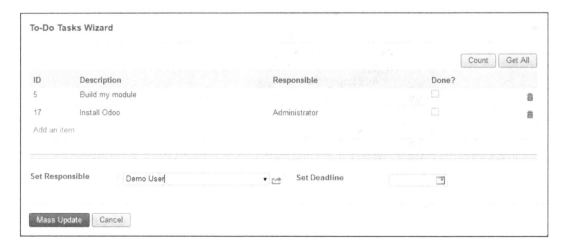

Wizard business logic

Next we need to implement the actions performed while clicking on the **Mass Update** button. The method called by the button is `do_mass_update` and it should be defined in the `todo_wizard/todo_wizard_model.py` file, as shown in the following code:

```
@api.multi
def do_mass_update(self):
    self.ensure_one()
    if not (self.new_deadline or self.new_user_id):
        raise exceptions.ValidationError('No data to update!')
    # else:
    _logger.debug('Mass update on Todo Tasks %s',
        self.task_ids.ids)
    if self.new_deadline:
        self.task_ids.write({'date_deadline': self.new_deadline})
    if self.new_user_id:
        self.task_ids.write({'user_id': self.new_user_id.id})
    return True
```

Our code can handle only one wizard instance at a time. We could have used `@api.one`, but it is not advised to do so in wizards. In some cases, we want the wizard to return a window action telling the client what to do next. That is not possible with `@api.one`, since it would return a list of actions instead of a single one.

Because of this, we prefer to use `@api.multi` but then we use `ensure_one()` to check that `self` represents a single record. It should be noted that `self` is a record representing the data on the wizard form.

The method begins by validating if a new deadline date or responsible user was given, and raises an error if not. Next, we demonstrate writing a message to the server log.

If the validation passes, we write the new values given to the selected tasks. We are using the `write` method on a record set, such as the `task_ids` to many field to perform a mass update. This is more efficient than repeating a write on each record in a loop.

Now we will work on the logic behind the two buttons at the top: **Count** and **Get All**.

Raising exceptions

When something is not right, we will want to interrupt the program with an error message. This is done by raising an exception. Odoo provides a few additional exception classes to the ones available in Python. These are examples for the most useful ones:

```
from openerp import exceptions
raise exceptions.Warning('Warning message')
raise exceptions.ValidationError('Not valid message')
```

The `Warning` message also interrupts execution but can sound less severe that a `ValidationError`. While it's not the best user interface, we take advantage of that on the **Count** button to display a message to the user:

```
@api.multi
def do_count_tasks(self):
    Task = self.env['todo.task']
    count = Task.search_count([])
    raise exceptions.Warning(
      'There are %d active tasks.' % count)
```

Auto-reloading code changes

When you're working on Python code, the server needs to be restarted every time the code is changed to reload it. To make life easier for developers an `--auto-reload` option is available. It monitors the source code and automatically reloads it if changes are detected. Here is an example of it's usage:

```
$ ./odoo.py -d v8dev --auto-reload
```

But this is a Linux-only feature. If you are using Debian/Ubuntu box to run the server, as recommended in *Chapter 1*, *Getting Started with Odoo Development*, it should work for you. The `pyinotify` Python package is required, and it should be installed either through `apt-get` or `pip`, as shown here:

```
$ sudo apt-get install python-pyinotify  # using OS packages
```

```
$ pip install pyinotify  # using pip, possibly in a virtualenv
```

Actions on the wizard dialog

Now suppose we want a button to automatically pick all the to-do tasks to spare the user from picking them one by one. That's the point of having the **Get All** button in the form. The code behind this button will get a record set with all active tasks and assign it to the tasks in the many to many field.

But there is a catch here. In dialog windows, when a button is pressed, the wizard window is automatically closed. We didn't face this problem on the `Count` button because it uses an exception to display it's message; so the action fails and the window is not closed.

Fortunately we can work around this behavior by returning an action to the client that reopens the same wizard. The model methods are allowed to return an action for the web client to perform, in the form of a dictionary describing the window action to execute. This dictionary uses the same attributes used to define window actions in module XML.

We will use a helper function for the window action dictionary to reopen the wizard window, so that it can be easily reused in several buttons, as shown here:

```
@api.multi
def do_reopen_form(self):
    self.ensure_one()
    return {
        'type': 'ir.actions.act_window',
        'res_model': self._name,  # this model
        'res_id': self.id,  # the current wizard record
        'view_type': 'form',
        'view_mode': 'form',
        'target': 'new'}
```

It is worth noting that the window action could be anything else, like jumping to a specific form and record, or opening another wizard form to ask for additional user input.

Now the **Get All** button can do its job and keep the user working on the same wizard:

```
@api.multi
def do_populate_tasks(self):
    self.ensure_one()
    Task = self.env['todo.task']
    all_tasks = Task.search([])
    self.task_ids = all_tasks
    # reopen wizard form on same wizard record
    return self.do_reopen_form()
```

Here we can see how to get a reference to a different model, which is `todo.task` in this case, to perform actions on it. The wizard form values are stored in the transient model and can be read and written as in regular models. We can also see that the method sets the `task_ids` value with the list of all active tasks.

Note that since `self` is not guaranteed to be a single record, we validate that using `self.ensure_one()`. We shouldn't use the `@api.one` decorator because it would wrap the returned value in a list. Since the web client expects to receive a dictionary and not a list, it wouldn't work as intended.

Working with the server

Our server code will usually run inside a method of a model, as is the case for `do_mass_update()` in the preceding code.

In this context, `self` represents the recordset being acted upon. Instances of model classes are actually recordsets. For actions executed from views, this will be only the record currently selected on it. If it's a form view, it is usually a single record, but in tree views, there can be several records.

The `self.env` object allows us to access our running environment; this includes the information on the current session, such as the current user and session context, and also access all the other models available in the server.

To better explore programming on the server side, we can use the server interactive console, where we have an environment similar to what we can find inside a model method.

This is a new feature for version 9. It has been back-ported as a module for version 8, and it can be downloaded from the link `https://www.odoo.com/apps/modules/8.0/shell/`. It just needs to be placed somewhere in your add-ons path, and no further installation is necessary, or you can use the following commands to get the code from GitHub and make the module available in our custom add-ons directory:

```
$ cd ~/odoo-dev
$ git clone https://github.com/OCA/server-tools.git -b 8.0
$ ln -s server-tools/shell custom-addons/shell
$ cd ~/odoo-dev/odoo
```

To use this, run `odoo.py` with the `shell` command and the database to use as shown here:

```
$ ./odoo.py shell -d v8dev
```

You will see the server start up sequence in the terminal ending in a `>>>` Python prompt. Here, `self` represents the record for the administrator user as shown here:

```
>>> self
res.users(1,)
>>> self.name
```

```
u'Administrator'
>>> self._name
'res.users'
>>> self.env
<openerp.api.Environment object at 0xb3f4f52c>
```

In the session above, we do some inspection on our environment. `self` represents a `res.users` recordset containing only the record with ID 1 and name Administrator. We can also confirm the recordset's model name inspecting `self._name`, and confirm that `self.env` is a reference for the environment.

As usual, you can exit the prompt using *Ctrl + D*. This will also close the server process and bring you back to the system shell prompt.

The `Model` class referenced by self is in fact a recordset, an iterable collection of records. Iterating through a recordset returns individual records.

The special case of a recordset with only one record is called a **singleton**. Singletons behave like records, and for all practical purposes are the same thing as a record. This particularity means that a record can be used wherever a recordset is expected.

Unlike multi-element recordsets, singletons can access their fields using the dot notation, as shown here:

```
>>> print self.name
Administrator
>>> for rec in self:
        print rec.name
Administrator
```

In this example, we loop through the records in the `self` recordset and print out the content of their `name` field. It contains only one record, so only one name is printed out. As you can see, `self` is a singleton and behaves as a record, but at the same time is iterable like a recordset.

Using relation fields

As we saw earlier, models can have relational fields: **many to one**, **one to many**, and **many to many**. These field types have recordsets as values.

In the case of many to one, the value can be a singleton or an empty recordset. In both cases, we can directly access their field values. As an example, the following instructions are correct and safe:

```
>>> self.company_id
res.company(1,)
>>> self.company_id.name
u'YourCompany'
>>> self.company_id.currency_id
res.currency(1,)
>>> self.company_id.currency_id.name
u'EUR'
```

Conveniently, an empty recordset also behaves like a singleton, and accessing its fields does not return an error but just returns `False`. Because of this, we can traverse records using dot notation without worrying about errors from empty values, as shown here:

```
>>> self.company_id.country_id
res.country()
>>> self.company_id.country_id.name
False
```

Querying models

With `self` we can only access the method's recordset. But the `self.env` environment reference allows us to access any other model.

For example, `self.env['res.partner']` returns a reference to the Partners model (which is actually an empty recordset). We can then use `search()` or `browse()` on it to generate recordsets.

The `search()` method takes a domain expression and returns a recordset with the records matching those conditions. An empty domain `[]` will return all records. If the model has the `active` special field, by default only the records with `active=True` will be considered. A few optional keyword arguments are available, as shown here:

- `order`: This is a string to be used as the ORDER BY clause in the database query. This is usually a comma-separated list of field names.

- `limit`: This sets a maximum number of records to retrieve.

- `offset`: This ignores the first n results; it can be used with limit to query blocks of records at a time.

Sometimes we just need to know the number of records meeting certain conditions. For that we can use `search_count()`, which returns the record count instead of a recordset.

The `browse()` method takes a list of IDs or a single ID and returns a recordset with those records. This can be convenient for the cases where we already know the IDs of the records we want.

Some usage examples of this are shown here:

```
>>> self.env['res.partner'].search([('name', 'like', 'Ag')])
res.partner(7, 51)
>>> self.env['res.partner'].browse([7, 51])
res.partner(7, 51)
```

Writing on records

Recordsets implement the active record pattern. This means that we can assign values on them, and these changes will be made persistent in the database. This is an intuitive and convenient way to manipulate data, as shown here:

```
>>> admin = self.env['res.users'].browse(1)
>>> admin.name = 'Superuser'
>>> print admin.name
Superuser
```

Recordsets have three methods to act on their data: `create()`, `write()`, and `unlink()`.

The `create()` method takes a dictionary to map fields to values and returns the created record. Default values are automatically applied as expected, which is shown here:

```
>>> Partner = self.env['res.partner']
>>> new = Partner.create({'name': 'ACME', 'is_company': True})
>>> print new
res.partner(72,)
```

The `unlink()` method deletes the records in the recordset, as shown here:

```
>>> rec = Partner.search([('name', '=', 'ACME')])
>>> rec.unlink()
True
```

The `write()` method takes a dictionary to map fields to values. These are updated on all elements of the recordset and nothing is returned, as shown here:

```
>>> Partner.write({'comment': 'Hello!'})
```

Using the active record pattern has some limitations; it updates only one field at a time. On the other hand, the `write()` method can update several fields of several records at the same time by using a single database instruction. These differences should be kept in mind for the cases where performance can be an issue.

It is also worth mentioning `copy()` to duplicate an existing record; it takes that as an optional argument and a dictionary with the values to write on the new record. For example, to create a new user copying from the Demo User:

```
>>> demo = self.env.ref('base.user_demo')
>>> new = demo.copy({'name': 'Daniel', 'login': 'dr', 'email':''})
>>> self.env.cr.commit()
```

Remember that fields with the `copy=False` attribute won't be copied.

Transactions and low-level SQL

Database writing operations are executed in the context of a database transaction. Usually we don't have to worry about this as the server takes care of that while running model methods.

But in some cases, we may need a finer control over the transaction. This can be done through the database cursor `self.env.cr`, as shown here:

- `self.env.cr.commit()`: This commits the transaction's buffered write operations.
- `self.env.savepoint()`: This sets a transaction savepoint to rollback to.
- `self.env.rollback()`: This cancels the transaction's write operations since the last savepoint or all if no savepoint was created.

> In a shell session, your data manipulation won't be made effective in the database until you use `self.env.cr.commit()`.

With the cursor `execute()` method, we can run SQL directly in the database. It takes a string with the SQL statement to run and a second optional argument with a tuple or list of values to use as parameters for the SQL. These values will be used where `%s` placeholders are found.

If you're using a SELECT query, records should then be fetched. The `fetchall()` function retrieves all the rows as a list of `tuples` and `dictfetchall()` retrieves them as a list of dictionaries, as shown in the following example:

```
>>> self.env.cr.execute("SELECT id, login FROM res_users WHERE
    login=%s OR id=%s", ('demo', 1))
>>> self.env.cr.fetchall()
    [(4, u'demo'), (1, u'admin')]
```

It's also possible to run data manipulation language instructions (DML) such as UPDATE and INSERT. Since the server keeps data caches, they may become inconsistent with the actual data in the database. Because of that, while using raw DML, the caches should be cleared afterwards by using `self.env. invalidate_all()`.

> **Caution!**
> Executing SQL directly in the database can lead to inconsistent data. You should use it only if you are sure of what you are doing.

Working with time and dates

For historical reasons, date and datetime values are handled as strings instead of the corresponding Python types. Also datetimes are stored in the database in UTC time. The formats used in the string representation are defined by:

- `openerp.tools.misc.DEFAULT_SERVER_DATE_FORMAT`
- `openerp.tools.misc.DEFAULT_SERVER_DATETIME_FORMAT`

They map to `%Y-%m-%d` and `%Y-%m-%d %H:%M:%S` respectively.

To help handle dates, `fields.Date` and `fields.Datetime` provide a few functions. For example:

```
>>> from openerp import fields
>>> fields.Datetime.now()
'2014-12-08 23:36:09'
>>> fields.Datetime.from_string('2014-12-08 23:36:09')
    datetime.datetime(2014, 12, 8, 23, 36, 9)
```

Given that dates and times are handled and stored by the server in a naive UTC format, which is not time zone aware and is probably different from the time zone that the user is working on, a few other functions that help to deal with this are shown here:

- `fields.Date.today()`: This returns a string with the current date in the format expected by the server and using UTC as a reference. This is adequate to compute default values.

- `fields.Datetime.now()`: This returns a string with the current datetime in the format expected by the server using UTC as a reference. This is adequate to compute default values.

- `fields.Date.context_today(record, timestamp=None)`: This returns a string with the current date in the session's context. The timezone value is taken from the record's context, and the optional parameter to use is datetime instead of the current time.

- `fields.Datetime.context_timestamp(record, timestamp)`: That converts a naive datetime (without timezone) into a timezone aware datetime. The timezone is extracted from the record's context, hence the name of the function.

To facilitate conversion between formats, both `fields.Date` and `fields.Datetime` objects provide these functions:

- `from_string(value)`: This converts a string into a date or datetime object.

- `to_string(value)`: This converts a date or datetime object into a string in the format expected by the server.

Working with relation fields

While using the active record pattern, relational fields can be assigned recordsets.

For a many to one field, the value assigned must be a single record (a singleton recordset).

For to-many fields, their value can also be assigned with a recordset, replacing the list of linked records, if any, with a new one. Here a recordset with any size is allowed.

While using the `create()` or `write()` methods, where values are assigned using dictionaries, relational fields can't be assigned to recordset values. The corresponding ID, or list of IDs should be used.

For example, instead of `self.write({'user_id': self.env.user})`, we should rather use `self.write({'user_id': self.env.user.id})`.

Manipulating recordsets

We will surely want to add, remove, or replace the elements in these related fields, and so this leads to the question: how can recordsets be manipulated?

Recordsets are immutable but can be used to compose new recordsets. Some set operations are supported, which are shown here:

- `rs1 | rs2`: This results in a recordset with all elements from both recordsets.
- `rs1 + rs2`: This also concatenates both recordsets into one.
- `rs1 & rs2`: This results in a recordset with only the elements present in both recordsets.
- `rs1 - rs2`: This results in a recordset with the `rs1` elements not present in `rs2`.

The slice notation can also be used, as shown here:

- `rs[0]` and `rs[-1]` retrieve the first element and the last elements.
- `rs[1:]` results in a copy of the recordset without the first element. This yields the same records as `rs - rs[0]` but preserves their order.

In general, while manipulating recordsets, you should assume that the record order is not preserved. However, addition and slicing are known to keep record order.

We can use these recordset operations to change the list by removing or adding elements. You can see this in the following example:

- `self.task_ids |= task1`: This adds task1 element if it's not in the recordset.
- `self.task_ids -= task1`: This removes the reference to task1 if it's present in the recordset.
- `self.task_ids = self.task_ids[:-1]`: This unlinks the last record.

While using the `create()` and `write()` methods with values in a dictionary, a special syntax is used to modify to many fields. This was explained in *Chapter 4, Data Serialization and Module Data*, in the section *Setting values for relation fields*. Refer to the following sample operations equivalent to the preceding ones using `write()`:

- `self.write([(4, task1.id, False)])`: This adds task1 to the member.
- `self.write([(3, task1.id, False)])`: This unlinks task1.
- `self.write([(3, self.task_ids[-1].id, False)])`: This unlinks the last element.

Other recordset operations

Recordsets support additional operations on them.

We can check if a record is included or is not in a recordset by doing the following:

- `record in recordset`
- `record not in recordset`

These operations are also available:

- `recordset.ids`: This returns the list with the IDs of the recordset elements.
- `recordset.ensure_one()`: This checks if it is a single record (singleton); if it's not, it raises a ValueError exception.
- `recordset.exists()`: This returns a copy with only the records that still exist.
- `recordset.filtered(func)`: This returns a filtered recordset.
- `recordset.mapped(func)`: This returns a list of mapped values.
- `recordset.sorted(func)`: This returns an ordered recordset.

Here are some usage examples for these functions:

```
>>> rs0 = self.env['res.partner'].search([])
>>> len(rs0)   # how many records?
68
>>> rs1 = rs0.filtered(lambda r: r.name.startswith('A'))
>>> print rs1
res.partner(3, 7, 6, 18, 51, 58, 39)
>>> rs2 = rs1.filtered('is_company')
>>> print rs2
res.partner(7, 6, 18)
>>> rs2.mapped('name')
[u'Agrolait', u'ASUSTeK', u'Axelor']
>>> rs2.mapped(lambda r: (r.id, r.name))
[(7, u'Agrolait'), (6, u'ASUSTeK'), (18, u'Axelor')]
>> rs2.sorted(key=lambda r: r.id, reverse=True)
res.partner(18, 7, 6)
```

The execution environment

The environment provides contextual information used by the server. Every recordset carries its execution environment in `self.env` with these attributes:

- `env.cr`: This is the database cursor being used.
- `env.uid`: This is the ID for the session user.
- `env.user`: This is the record for the session user.
- `env.context`: This is an immutable dictionary with a session context.

The environment is immutable, and so it can't be modified. But we can create modified environments and then run actions using them. These methods can be used for that:

- `env.sudo(user)`: If this is provided with a user record, it returns an environment with that user. If no user is provided, the administrator superuser will be used, which allows running specific queries bypassing security rules.
- `env.with_context(dictionary)`: This replaces the context with a new one.
- `env.with_context(key=value, ...)`: This sets values for keys in the current context.

The `env.ref()` function takes a string with an External ID and returns a record for it, as shown here:

```
>>> self.env.ref('base.user_root')
res.users(1,)
```

Model methods for client interaction

We have seen the most important model methods used to generate recordsets and how to write on them. But there are a few more model methods available for more specific actions, as shown here:

- `read([fields])`: This is similar to browse, but instead of a recordset, it returns a list of rows of data with the fields given as it's argument. Each row is a dictionary. It provides a serialized representation of the data that can be sent through RPC protocols and is intended to be used by client programs and not in server logic.

- `search_read([domain], [fields], offset=0, limit=None, order=None)`: This performs a search operation followed by a read on the resulting record list. It is intended to be used by RPC clients and saves them the extra round trip needed when doing a search first and then a read.

- `load([fields], [data])`: This is used to import data acquired from a CSV file. The first argument is the list of fields to import, and it maps directly to a CSV top row. The second argument is a list of records, where each record is a list of string values to parse and import, and it maps directly to the CSV data rows and columns. It implements the features of CSV data import described in *Chapter 4, Data Serialization and Module Data*, like the External IDs support. It is used by the web client Import feature. It replaces the deprecated `import_data` method.

- `export_data([fields], raw_data=False)`: This is used by the web client Export function. It returns a dictionary with a data key containing the data–a list of rows. The field names can use the `.id` and `/id` suffixes used in CSV files, and the data is in a format compatible with an importable CSV file. The optional `raw_data` argument allows for data values to be exported with their Python types, instead of the string representation used in CSV.

The following methods are mostly used by the web client to render the user interface and perform basic interaction:

- `name_get()`: This returns a list of (ID, name) tuples with the text representing each record. It is used by default to compute the `display_name` value, providing the text representation of relation fields. It can be extended to implement custom display representations, such as displaying the record code and name instead of only the name.

- `name_search(name='', args=None, operator='ilike', limit=100)`: This also returns a list of (ID, name) tuples, where the display name matches the text in the name argument. It is used by the UI while typing in a relation field to produce the list suggested records matching the typed text. It is used to implement product lookup both by name and by reference while typing in a field to pick a product.

- `name_create(name)`: This creates a new record with only the title name to use for it. It is used by the UI for the quick-create feature, where you can quickly create a related record by just providing its name. It can be extended to provide specific defaults while creating new records through this feature.

- `default_get([fields])`: This returns a dictionary with the default values for a new record to be created. The default values may depend on variables such as the current user or the session context.

- `fields_get()`: This is used to describe the model's field definitions, as seen in the **View Fields** option of the developer menu.

- `fields_view_get()`: This is used by the web client to retrieve the structure of the UI view to render. It can be given the ID of the view as an argument or the type of view we want using `view_type='form'`. Look at an example of this: `rset.fields_view_get(view_type='tree')`.

Overriding the default methods

We have learned about the standard methods provided by the API. But what we can do with them doesn't end there! We can also extend them to add custom behavior to our models.

The most common case is to extend the `create()` and `write()` methods. This can be used to add the logic triggered whenever these actions are executed. By placing our logic in the appropriate section of the custom method, we can have the code run before or after the main operations are executed.

Using the `TodoTask` model as an example, we can make a custom `create()`, which would look like this:

```
@api.model
def create(self, vals):
    # Code before create
    # Can use the `vals` dict
    new_record = super(TodoTask, self).create(vals)
    # Code after create
    # Can use the `new` record created
    return new_record
```

A custom `write()` would follow this structure:

```
@api.multi
def write(self, vals):
    # Code before write
    # Can use `self`, with the old values
    super(TodoTask, self).write(vals)
    # Code after write
    # Can use `self`, with the new (updated) values
    return True
```

These are common extension examples, but of course any standard method available for a model can be inherited in a similar way to add to it our custom logic.

These techniques open up a lot of possibilities, but remember that other tools are also available that are better suited for common specific tasks and should be preferred:

- To have a field value calculated based on another, we should use computed fields. An example of this is to calculate a total when the values of the lines are changed.

- To have field default values calculated dynamically, we can use a field default bound to a function instead of a scalar value.

- To have values set on other fields when a field is changed, we can use on-change functions. An example of this is when picking a customer to set the document's currency to the corresponding partner's, which can afterwards be manually changed by the user. Keep in mind that on-change only works on form view interaction and not on direct write calls.

- For validations, we should use constraint functions decorated with `@api.constrains(fld1,fld2,...)`. These are like computed fields but are expected to raise errors when conditions are not met instead of computing values.

Model method decorators

During our journey, the several methods we encountered used API decorators like `@api.one`. These are important for the server to know how to handle the method. We have already given some explanation of the decorators used; now let's recap the ones available and when they should be used:

- `@api.one`: This feeds one record at a time to the function. The decorator does the recordset iteration for us and `self` is guaranteed to be a singleton. It's the one to use if our logic only needs to work with each record. It also aggregates the return values of the function on each record in a list, which can have unintended side effects.

- `@api.multi`: This handles a recordset. We should use it when our logic can depend on the whole recordset and seeing isolated records is not enough, or when we need a return value that is not a list like a dictionary with a window action. In practice it is the one to use most of the time as `@api.one` has some overhead and list wrapping effects on result values.

- `@api.model`: This is a class-level static method, and it does not use any recordset data. For consistency, `self` is still a recordset, but its content is irrelevant.

- `@api.returns(model)`: This indicates that the method return instances of the model in the argument, such as `res.partner` or `self` for the current model.

The decorators that have more specific purposes that were explained in detail in *Chapter 5, Models – Structuring Application Data* are shown here:

- `@api.depends(fld1,...)`: This is used for computed field functions to identify on what changes the (re)calculation should be triggered.
- `@api.constrains(fld1,...)`: This is used for validation functions to identify on what changes the validation check should be triggered.
- `@api.onchange(fld1,...)`: This is used for on-change functions to identify the fields on the form that will trigger the action.

In particular the on-change methods can send a warning message to the user interface. For example, this could warn the user that the product quantity just entered is not available on stock, without preventing the user from continuing. This is done by having the method return a dictionary describing the following warning message:

```
return {
    'warning': {
        'title': 'Warning!',
        'message': 'The warning text'}
}
```

Debugging

We all know that a good part of a developer's work is to debug code. To do this we often make use of a code editor that can set breakpoints and run our program step by step. Doing so with Odoo is possible, but it has it's challenges.

If you're using Microsoft Windows as your development workstation, setting up an environment capable of running Odoo code from source is a nontrivial task. Also the fact that Odoo is a server that waits for client calls and only then acts on them makes it quite different to debug compared to client-side programs.

While this can certainly be done with Odoo, arguably it might not be the most pragmatic approach to the issue. We will introduce some basic debugging strategies, which can be as effective as many sophisticated IDEs with some practice.

Python's integrated debug tool pdb can do a decent job at debugging. We can set a breakpoint by inserting the following line in the desired place:

```
import pdb; pdb.set_trace()
```

Now restart the server so that the modified code is loaded. As soon as the program execution reaches that line, a (pdb) Python prompt will be shown in the terminal window where the server is running, waiting for our input.

This prompt works as a Python shell, where you can run any expression or command in the current execution context. This means that the current variables can be inspected and even modified. These are the most important shortcut commands available:

- h: This is used to display a help summary of the pdb commands.
- p: This is used to to evaluate and print an expression.
- pp: This is for pretty print, which is useful for larger dictionaries or lists.
- l: This lists the code around the instruction to be executed next.
- n (next): This steps over to the next instruction.
- s (step): This steps into the current instruction.
- c (continue): This continues execution normally.
- u(up): This allows to move up the execution stack.
- d(down): This allows to move down the execution stack.

The Odoo server also supports the --debug option. If it's used, when the server finds an exception, it enters into a *post mortem* mode at the line where the error was raised. This is a pdb console and it allows us to inspect the program state at the moment where the error was found.

It's worth noting that there are alternatives to the Python built-in debugger. There is pudb that supports the same commands as pdb and works in text-only terminals, but uses a more friendly graphical display, making useful information readily available such as the variables in the current context and their values.

```
PuDB 2013.3.6 - ?:help  n:next  s:step into  b:breakpoint  o:output  t:run to cursor  !:python shell
  1 from openerp import models, fields, api                      Variables:
  2 from openerp import exceptions                               pp: <function pprint at 0x1897
  3                                                                   0c8>
  4                                                              pudb: <module 'pudb' from '/us
  5                                                                   r/local/lib/python2.7/dist-p
  6                                                                   ackages/pudb/__init__.pyc'>
  7 class TodoWizard(models.TransientModel):                     result: True
  8     _name =                                                  self: todo.wizard(11,)
  9     new_user = fields.Many2one(          , string=
 10     new_deadline = fields.Date(              )
 11     tasks = fields.Many2many(          , string=        )
 12
 13     @api.one
 14     def button_test(self):
 15         result = True
 16         from pprint import pprint as pp
 17         import pudb; pudb.set_trace()
> 18
 19
 20     @api.one
 21     def do_populate(self):
 22         Todo = self.env[          ]
 23         all_todos = Todo.search([])
 24         #self.tasks = all_todos                             Stack:
 25         # Reopen wizard                                                    [todo.wizard]
 26         action = {                                           new_api [todo.wizard]
 27                          :              ,                    old_api [todo.wizard]
 28                          :              ,                    wrapper [todo.wizard]
 29                          :              ,                  Breakpoints:
 30             #'res_id': self.id,
 31                          :              , #self._name,
 32                          :              ,
 33         }
```

It can be installed either through the system package manager or through pip, as shown here:

```
$ sudo apt-get install python-pudb  # using OS packages
$ pip install pudb  # using pip, possibly in a virtualenv
```

It works just like `pdb`; you just need to use `pudb` instead of `pdb` in the breakpoint code.

Another option is the Iron Python debugger `ipdb`, which can be installed by using the following code:

```
$ pip install ipdb
```

Sometimes we just need to inspect the values of some variables or check if some code blocks are being executed. A Python `print` statement can perfectly do the job without stopping the execution flow. As we are running the server in a terminal window, the printed text will be shown in the standard output. But it won't be stored to the server log if it's being written to a file.

Another option to keep in mind is to set debug level log messages at sensitive points of our code if we feel that we might need them to investigate issues in a deployed instance. It would only be needed to elevate that server logging level to DEBUG and then inspect the log files.

Summary

In the previous chapters, you saw how to build models and design views. Here you went a little further learning how to implement business logic and use recordsets to manipulate model data.

You also saw how the business logic can interact with the user interface and learned to create wizards that dialogue with the user and serve as a platform to launch advanced processes.

In the next chapter, our focus will go back to the user interface, and you will learn how to create powerful kanban views and design your own business reports.

8

QWeb – Creating Kanban Views and Reports

QWeb is a template engine used by Odoo. It is XML based and is used to generate HTML fragments and pages. QWeb was first introduced in version 7.0 to enable richer kanban views, and with version 8.0, is also used for report generation and CMS website pages.

Here you will learn about the QWeb syntax and how to use it to create your own kanban views and custom reports.

To understand kanban boards, **kanban** is a word of Japanese origin that is used to represent a work queue management method. It takes inspiration from the Toyota Production System and Lean Manufacturing, and has become popular in the software industry with its adoption in Agile methodologies.

The **kanban board** is a tool to visualize the work queue. Work items are represented by **cards** that are organized in columns representing the **stages** of the work process. New work items start on the left-most column and travel through the board until they reach the right-most column, representing completed work.

Getting started with kanban board

The simplicity and visual impact of kanban board make them excellent to support simple business processes. A basic example of a kanban board can have three columns, as shown in the following image: "To Do," "Doing," and "Done," but it can of course be extended to whatever specific process steps we may need:

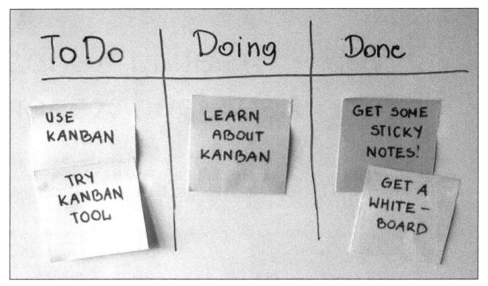

Photo credits: A Scrum board suggesting using kanban by Jeff.lasovski. Courtesy of Wikipedia.

Kanban views are a distinctive Odoo feature, making it easy to implement these boards. Let's learn how to use them.

Kanban views

In form views, we use mostly specific XML elements, such as `<field>` and `<group>`, and few HTML elements, such as `<h1>` or `<div>`. With kanban views, it's quite the opposite; they are HTML-based templates and support only two Odoo-specific elements, `<field>` and `<button>`.

The HTML can be dynamically generated using the QWeb template engine. It processes special tag attributes in HTML elements to produce the final HTML to be presented in the web client. This brings a lot of control on how to render the content, but also make view design a more complex.

Kanban views are so flexible that there can be many different ways to design them, and it can be hard to provide a recipe to follow. A good rule of thumb is to find an existing kanban view similar to what we want to achieve, and create our new kanban view work based on it.

Looking at the kanban views used in the standard modules, it's possible to identify two main kanban view styles: vignette and card kanbans.

Examples of **vignette** style kanban views can be found for **Customers**, **Products**, and also **Apps & Modules**. They usually have no border and are decorated with an image on the left-hand side, as shown in the following image:

The **card** style kanban is usually used to display cards organized in columns for the process stages. Examples are **CRM Opportunities** and **Project Tasks**. The main content is displayed in the card top area and additional information can be displayed in the bottom-right and bottom-left areas, as shown in the following image:

We will see the skeleton and typical elements used in both styles of views so that you can feel comfortable adapting them to your particular use cases.

Design kanban views

First thing is to create a new module adding our kanban views to to-do tasks. In a real-world work, situation using a module for this would probably be excessive and they could perfectly well be added directly in the todo_ui module. But for a clearer explanation, we will use a new module and avoid too many, and possibly confusing, changes in already created files. We will name it todo_kanban and create the usual initial files as follows:

```
$ cd ~/odoo-dev/custom-addons
$ mkdir todo_kanban
$ touch todo_kanban/__init__.py
```

Now, edit the descriptor file todo_kanban/__openerp__.py as follows:

```
{'name': 'To-Do Kanban',
 'description': 'Kanban board for to-do tasks.',
 'author': 'Daniel Reis',
 'depends': ['todo_ui'],
 'data': ['todo_view.xml'] }
```

Next, create the XML file where our shiny new kanban views will go and set kanban as the default view on the to-do task's window action, as shown in the following:

```
<?xml version="1.0"?>
<openerp>
  <data>
    <!-- Add Kanban view mode to the menu Action: -->
    <act_window id="todo_app.action_todo_task"
        name=" To-Do Tasks"
        res_model="todo.task"
        view_mode="kanban,tree,form,calendar,gantt,graph"
        context="{'search_default_filter_my_tasks': True}" />
    <!-- Add Kanban view -->
    <record id="To-do Task Kanban" model="ir.ui.view">
      <field name="name">To-do Task Kanban</field>
      <field name="model">todo.task</field>
      <field name="arch" type="xml">
        <!-- Empty for now, but the Kanban will go here! -->
      </field>
    </record>
  </data>
</openerp>
```

Now we have in place the basic skeleton for our module. The templates used in kanban views and reports are extended using the regular techniques used for other views, for example using XPATH expressions. See *Chapter 3, Inheritance – Extending Existing Applications*, for more details.

Before starting with the kanban views, we need to add a couple of fields to the to-do tasks model.

Priority and kanban state

The two fields that are frequently used in kanban views are priority and kanban state. **Priority** lets users organize their work items, signaling what should be addressed first. **Kanban state** signals whether a task is ready to move to the next stage or is blocked for some reason. Both are supported by selection fields and have specific widgets to use on forms and kanban views.

To add these fields to our model, we will add a `todo_kanban/todo_model.py` file, as shown in the following:

```
from openerp import models, fields
class TodoTask(models.Model):
    _inherit = 'todo.task'
    priority = fields.Selection(
        [('0', 'Low'), ('1', 'Normal'), ('2', 'High')],
        'Priority', default='1')
    kanban_state = fields.Selection(
        [('normal', 'In Progress'),
         ('blocked', 'Blocked'),
         ('done', 'Ready for next stage')],
        'Kanban State', default='normal')
```

Let's not forget the `todo_kanban/__init__.py` file that will load the preceding code:

```
from . import todo_task
```

Kanban view elements

The kanban view architecture has a `<kanban>` top element and the following basic structure:

```
<kanban>
  <!-- Fields to use in expressions... -->
  <field name="a_field" />
  <templates>
    <t t-name="kanban-box">
```

```
      <!-- HTML Qweb template ... -->
    </t>
  </templates>
</kanban>
```

The `<templates>` element contains the templates for the HTML fragments to use—one or more. The main template to be used must be named `kanban-box`. Other templates are allowed for HTML fragments to include in the main template.

The templates use standard HTML, but can include the `<field>` tag to insert model fields. Some QWeb special directives for dynamic content generation can also be used, like the `t-name` used in the previous example.

All model fields used have to be declared with a `<field>` tag. If they are used only in expressions, we have to declare them before the `<templates>` section. One of these fields is allowed to have an aggregated value, displayed at the top of the kanban columns. This is done by adding an attribute with the aggregation to use, for example:

```
<field name="effort_estimate" sum="Total Effort" />
```

Here the sum for the estimated effort field is presented at the top of the kanban columns with the label text **Total Effort**. Supported aggregations are `sum`, `avg`, `min`, `max`, and `count`.

The `<kanban>` top element also supports a few interesting attributes:

- `default_group_by`: This sets the field to use for the default column groups.
- `default_order`: This sets a default order to use for the kanban items.
- `quick_create="false"`: This disables the quick create option on the kanban view.
- `class`: This adds a CSS class to the root element of the rendered kanban view.

Now let's have a closer look at the QWeb templates to use in the kanban views.

The vignette kanban view

For the vignette kanban QWeb templates, the skeleton looks like the following:

```
<t t-name="kanban-box">
    <div class="oe_kanban_vignette">
        <!-- Left side image: -->
        <img class="oe_kanban_image" name="..." />
        <div class="oe_kanban_details">
```

```
        <!-- Title and data -->
        <h4>Title</h4>
        Other data <br/>
        <ul>
            <li>More data</li>
        </ul>
    </div>
  </div>
</t>
```

You can see the two main CSS classes provided for vignette style kanbans: oe_kanban_vignette for the top container and oe_kanban_details for the data content.

The complete vignette kanban view for the to-do tasks is as follows:

```
<kanban>
  <templates>
    <t t-name="kanban-box">
      <div class="oe_kanban_vignette">
        <img t-att-src="kanban_image('res.partner',
            'image_medium', record.id.value)"
            class="oe_kanban_image"/>
        <div class="oe_kanban_details">
          <!-- Title and Data content -->
          <h4><a type="open">
            <field name="name" />
          </a></h4>
          <field name="tag_ids" />
          <ul>
            <li><field name="user_id" /></li>
            <li><field name="date_deadline" /></li>
          </ul>
          <field name="kanban_state"
                 widget="kanban_state_selection"/>
          <field name="priority" widget="priority"/>
        </div>
      </div>
    </t>
  </templates>
</kanban>
```

We can see the elements discussed until now, and also a few new ones. In the <img> tag, we have the special t-att-src QWeb attribute. It can calculate the image src content from a database stored field. We will be explaining this and other QWeb directives in a moment. We can also see the usage of the special type attribute in the <a> tag. Let's have a closer look at it.

Actions in kanban views

In QWeb templates, the `<a>` tag for links can have a `type` attribute. It sets the type of action the link will perform so that links can act just like the buttons in regular forms. So in addition to the `<button>` elements, the `<a>` tags can also be used to run Odoo actions.

As in form views, the action type can be `action` or `object`, and it should be accompanied by a `name` attribute, identifying the specific action to execute. Additionally, the following action types are also available:

- `open`: This opens the corresponding form view.
- `edit`: This opens the corresponding form view directly in edit mode.
- `delete`: This deletes the record and removes the item from the kanban view.

The card kanban view

The **card** kanban can be a little more complex. It has a main content area and two footer sub-containers, aligned to each of the card sides. A button opening an action menu may also be featured at the card's top-right corner.

The skeleton for this template looks like the following:

```
<t t-name="kanban-box">
    <div class="oe_kanban_card">
        <div class="oe_dropdown_kanban oe_dropdown_toggle">
            <!-- Top-right drop down menu -->
        </div>
        <div class="oe_kanban_content">
            <!-- Content fields go here... -->
            <div class="oe_kanban_bottom_right"></div>
            <div class="oe_kanban_footer_left"></div>
        </div>
    </div>
</t>
```

A **card** kanban is more appropriate for the to-do tasks, so instead of the view described in the previous section, we would be better using the following:

```
<t t-name="kanban-box">
    <div class="oe_kanban_card">
        <div class="oe_kanban_content">
            <!-- Option menu will go here! -->
```

```
            <h4><a type="open">
                <field name="name" />
            </a></h4>
            <field name="tags" />
            <ul>
                <li><field name="user_id" /></li>
                <li><field name="date_deadline" /></li>
            </ul>
            <div class="oe_kanban_bottom_right">
                <field name="kanban_state"
                        widget="kanban_state_selection"/>
            </div>
            <div class="oe_kanban_footer_left">
                <field name="priority" widget="priority"/>
            </div>
        </div>
    </div>
</t>
```

So far we have seen static kanban views, using a combination of HTML and special tags (field, button, a). But we can have much more interesting results using dynamically generated HTML content. Let's see how we can do that using QWeb.

Adding QWeb dynamic content

The QWeb parser looks for special attributes (directives) in the templates and replaces them with dynamically generated HTML.

For kanban views, the parsing is done by client-side JavaScript. This means that the expression evaluations done by QWeb should be written using the JavaScript syntax, not Python.

When displaying a kanban view, the internal steps are roughly as follows:

- Get the XML for the templates to render.
- Call the server read() method to get the data for the fields in the templates.
- Locate the kanban-box template and parse it using QWeb to output the final HTML fragments.
- Inject the HTML in the browser's display (the DOM).

This is not meant to be technically exact. It is just a mind map that can be useful to understand how things work in kanban views.

Next we will explore the several QWeb directives available, using examples that enhance our to-do task kanban card.

Conditional rendering with t-if

The t-if directive, accepts a JavaScript expression to be evaluated. The tag and its content will be rendered if the condition evaluates to true.

For example, in the card kanban, to display the Task effort estimate, only if it has a value, after the date_deadline field, add the following:

```
<t t-if="record.effort_estimate.raw_value > 0">
    <li>Estimate <field name="effort_estimate"/></li>
</t>
```

The JavaScript evaluation context has a record object representing the record being rendered, with the fields requested from the server. The field values can be accessed using either the raw_value or the value attributes:

- raw_value: This is the value returned by the read() server method, so it's more suitable to use in condition expressions.

- value: This is formatted according to the user settings, and is meant to be used for display in the user interface.

The QWeb evaluation context also has references available for the JavaScript web client instance. To make use of them, a good understanding of the web client architecture is needed, but we won't be able to go into that detail. For reference purposes, the following identifiers are available in QWeb expression evaluation:

- widget: This is a reference to the current KanbanRecord widget object, responsible for the rendering of the current record into a kanban card. It exposes some useful helper functions we can use.

- record: This is a shortcut for widget.records and provides access to the fields available, using dot notation.

- read_only_mode: This indicates if the current view is in read mode (and not in edit mode). It is a shortcut for widget.view.options.read_only_mode.

- instance: This is a reference to the full web client instance.

It is also noteworthy that some characters are not allowed inside expressions. The lower than sign (<) is such a case. You may use a negated >= instead. Anyway, alternative symbols are available for inequality operations as follows:

- lt: This is for less than.

- lte: This is for less than or equal to.

- gt: This is for greater than.

- gte: This is for greater than or equal to.

Rendering values with t-esc and t-raw

We have used the `<field>` element to render the field content. But field values can also be presented directly without a `<field>` tag. The `t-esc` directive evaluates an expression and renders its HTML escaped value, as shown in the following:

```
<t t-esc="record.message_follower_ids.raw_value" />
```

In some cases, and if the source data is ensured to be safe, `t-raw` can be used to render the field raw value, without any escaping, as shown in the following code:

```
<t t-raw="record.message_follower_ids.raw_value" />
```

Loop rendering with t-foreach

A block of HTML can be repeated by iterating through a loop. We can use it to add the avatars of the task followers to the task's kanban card.

Let's start by rendering just the Partner IDs of the task, as follows:

```
<t t-foreach="record.message_follower_ids.raw_value" t-as="rec">
    <t t-esc="rec" />;
</t>
```

The `t-foreach` directive accepts a JavaScript expression evaluating to a collection to iterate. In most cases, this will be just the name of a *to many* relation field. It is used with a `t-as` directive to set the name to be used to refer to each item in the iteration.

In the previous example, we loop through the task followers, stored in the `message_follower_ids` field. Since there is limited space on the kanban card, we could have used the `slice()` JavaScript function to limit the number of followers to display, as shown in the following:

```
t-foreach="record.message_follower_ids.raw_value.slice(0, 3)"
```

The `rec` variable holds each iteration's value, a Partner ID in this case.

A few helper variables are also automatically created. They have the name defined in `t-as` as prefix. In our example we used `rec`, so the helper variables available are as follows:

- `rec_index`: This is the iteration index, starting from zero.
- `rec_size`: This is the number of elements of the collection.
- `rec_first`: This is true on the first element of the iteration.
- `rec_last`: This is true on the last element of the iteration.
- `rec_even`: This is true on even indexes.

- rec_odd: This is true on odd indexes.

- rec_parity: This is either odd or even, depending on the current index.

- rec_all: This represents the object being iterated over.

- rec_value: This, when iterating through a dictionary, {key: value}, holds the value (rec holds the key name).

For example, we could make use of the following to avoid a trailing comma on our ID list:

```
<t t-foreach="record.message_follower_ids.raw_value.slice(0, 3)"
   t-as="rec">
      <t t-esc="rec" /><t t-if="!rec_last">;</t>
</t>
```

Dynamic attributes with t-att- prefixes

We need to render the image for each follower. The final HTML would be something like <img src="URL" />, where the URL needs to be dynamically generated. QWeb can do this using t-att- prefixed directives. In this case, the src attribute can be rendered using a t-att-src directive with a JavaScript expression.

We also need to access the Partner's avatar stored in the database. Kanban views provide a helper function to conveniently generate that: kanban_image(). It accepts as arguments the model name, the field name holding the image we want, and the ID for the record to retrieve.

With this, we can rewrite the followers loop as follows:

```
<div>
   <t t-foreach="record.message_follower_ids.raw_value.slice(0, 3)"
      t-as="rec">
    <img t-att-src="kanban_image(
                    'res.partner', 'image_small', rec)"
        class="oe_kanban_image oe_kanban_avatar_smallbox"/>
   </t>
</div>
```

We used it for the src attribute, but any attribute can be dynamically generated with a t-att- prefix.

String substitution in attributes with t-attf- prefixes

Another way to dynamically generate tag attributes is using string substitution. This is helpful to have parts of larger strings generated dynamically, such as a URL address or CSS class names.

The directive contains expression blocks that will be evaluated and replaced by the result. These are delimited either by {{ and }} or by #{ and }. The content of the blocks can be any valid JavaScript expression and can use any of the variables available for QWeb expressions, such as `record` and `widget`.

Now let's replace `<field name="date_deadline"/>` in our kanban card with the following:

```
<span t-attf-class="oe_kanban_text{{
    record.date_deadline.raw_value and
    !(record.date_deadline.raw_value > (new Date()))
    ? '_red' : '_black' }}">
    <field name="date_deadline"/>
</span>
```

This results in either `class="oe_kanban_text_red"` or `class="oe_kanban_text_black"`, depending on the deadline date. Please note that, while the `oe_kanban_text_red` CSS class is available in kanban views, the `oe_kanban_text_black` CSS class does not exist and was used to better explain the point.

 The lower than sign (<) is not allowed in the expressions, and we chose to work around this by using a negated greater than comparison. Another possibility would be to use the `lt` (lower than) symbol instead.

Setting variables with t-set

For more complex logic, we can store the result of an expression into a variable to be used later in the template. This is to be done using the `t-set` directive, naming the variable to set, followed by the `t-value` directive, with the expression calculating the assigned value.

As an example, the following code renders missed deadlines in red, just as in the previous section, but uses a variable with the CSS class to use, as shown in the following:

```
<t t-set="red_or_black" t-value="
    record.date_deadline.raw_value and
    record.date_deadline.raw_value lte (new Date())
    ? 'oe_kanban_text_red' : ''" />
<span t-att-class="red_or_black">
    <field name="date_deadline" />
</span>
```

It is also possible to assign HTML content to a variable, as in the following example:

```
<t t-set="calendar_sign">
    <span class="oe_e">&#128197;</span>
</t>
<t t-raw="calendar_sign" />
```

The oe_e CSS class uses the Entypo pictogram font. The HTML representation for the calendar sign is stored in a variable that can then be used when needed in the template.

Calling other templates with t-call

We can have QWeb templates for HTML snippets that are reused in other templates. This makes it possible to have buildings blocks to use for composing the user interface views.

Additional templates are defined inside the `<templates>` tag and identified by a top element with a t-name other than kanban-box. A template can be included using the t-call directive.

The follower avatar list is something that could be isolated in a reusable snippet. Let's rework it to use a sub-template. We should start by adding another template to our XML file, inside the `<templates>` element, after the `<t t-name="kanban-box">` node, as shown in the following:

```
<t t-name="follower_avatars">
<div>
  <t t-foreach="record.message_follower_ids.raw_value.slice(0, 3)"
     t-as="rec">
    <img t-att-src="kanban_image(
         'res.partner', 'image_small', rec)"
         class="oe_kanban_image oe_kanban_avatar_smallbox"/>
  </t>
</div>
</t>
```

Calling it from the `kanban-box` main template is quite straightforward — instead of the `<div>` element containing the "for each" directive, we should use the following:

```
<t t-call="follower_avatars" />
```

We can also call templates defined in other modules. For this we just need to use the `module.name` full identifier, as we do with the other views. For instance, this snippet can be referred using the full identifier `todo_kanban.follower_avatars`.

The called template runs in the same context as the caller, so any variable names available in the caller are also available when processing the called template.

A more elegant solution is to pass arguments to the called template. This is done by setting variables inside the `t-call` tag. These will be evaluated and made available in the sub-template context only, and won't exist in the caller's context.

We could use this to have the maximum number of follower avatars set by the caller instead of being hard-coded in the sub-template. First, we need to replace the "3" fixed value by a variable, `arg_max` for example:

```
<t t-name="follower_avatars">
<div>
  <t t-foreach="record.message_follower_ids.raw_value.slice(
      0, arg_max)" t-as="rec">
    <img t-att-src="kanban_image(
          'res.partner', 'image_small', rec)"
          class="oe_kanban_image oe_kanban_avatar_smallbox"/>
  </t>
</div>
</t>
```

Then, define that variable's value when performing the sub-template call as follows:

```
<t t-call="follower_avatars">
    <t t-set="arg_max" t-value="3" />
</t>
```

The entire content inside the `t-call` element is also available to the sub-template through the magic variable `0`. Instead of the argument variables, we can define an HTML code fragment that could be inserted in the sub-template using `<t t-raw="0" />`.

Other QWeb directives

We have gone through through the most important QWeb directives, but there are a few more we should be aware of. We'll do a short explanation on them.

We have seen `t-att-NAME` and `t-attf-NAME` style dynamic tag attributes. Additionally, the fixed `t-att` directive can be used. It accepts either a key-value dictionary mapping or a pair (a two-element list).

Use the following mapping:

```
<p t-att="{'class': 'oe_bold', 'name': 'test1'}" />
```

This results in the following:

```
<p class="oe_bold" name="test1" />
```

Use the following pair:

```
<p t-att="['class', 'oe_bold']" />
```

This results in the following:

```
<p class="oe_bold" />
```

Advanced kanban elements

We've seen the basics about kanban views and QWeb templates. There are still a few techniques we can use to bring a richer user experience to our kanban cards.

Adding a kanban card option menu

Kanban cards can have an option menu, placed at the top right. Usual actions are to edit or delete the record, but any action callable from a button is possible. There is also available a widget to set the card's color.

The following is a baseline HTML code for the option menu to be added at the top of the `oe_kanban_content` element:

```
<div class="oe_dropdown_kanban oe_dropdown_toggle">
    <span class="oe_e">í</span>
    <ul class="oe_dropdown_menu">
        <t t-if="widget.view.is_action_enabled('edit')">
        <li><a type="edit">Edit...</a></li>
        </t>
```

```
        <t t-if="widget.view.is_action_enabled('delete')">
        <li><a type="delete">Delete</a></li>
        </t>
        <!-- Color picker option: -->
        <li><ul class="oe_kanban_colorpicker"
                data-field="color"/></li>
    </ul>
</div>
```

It is basically an HTML list of `<a>` elements. The **Edit** and **Delete** options use QWeb to make them visible only when their actions are enabled on the view. The `widget. view.is_action_enabled` function allows us to inspect if the edit and delete actions are available and to decide what to make available to the current user.

Adding colors to kanban cards

The color picker option allows the user to choose the color of a kanban card. The color is stored in a model field as a numeric index.

We should start by adding this field to the to-do task model, by adding to `todo_kanban/todo_model.py` the following line:

```
color = fields.Integer('Color Index')
```

Here we used the usual name for the field, `color`, and this is what is expected in the `data-field` attribute on the color picker.

Next, for the colors selected with the picker to have any effect on the card, we must add some dynamic CSS based on the `color` field value. On the kanban view, just before the `<templates>` tag, we must also declare the color field, as shown in the following:

```
<field name="color" />
```

And, we need to replace the kanban card top element, `<div class="oe_kanban_ card">`, with the following:

```
<div t-attf-class="oe_kanban_card
                    #{kanban_color(record.color.raw_value)}">
```

The `kanban_color` helper function does the translation of the color index into the corresponding CSS class name.

And that's it! You can now enjoy changing the kanban card colors at your will!

Using text ellipsis for long texts

Sometimes field texts may be too long to properly present in a kanban card. One way to avoid this is to cut the excessive text replacing it by an ellipsis (...). A helper function for this is available in kanban views.

For example, to limit our to-do task titles to the first 32 characters, we should replace the `<field name="name" />` element with the following:

```
<t t-esc="kanban_text_ellipsis(record.name.value, 32)" />
```

Custom CSS and JavaScript assets

As we have seen, kanban views are mostly HTML and make heavy use of CSS classes. We have been introducing some frequently used CSS classes provided by the standard product. But for best results, modules can also add their own CSS.

We are not going into details here on how to write CSS, but it's relevant to explain how a module can add its own CSS (and JavaScript) web assets. Odoo assets are declared in the `assets_backend` template. To add our module assets, we should extend that template. The XML file for this is usually placed inside a `views/` module subdirectory.

The following is a sample XML file to add a CSS and a JavaScript file to the `todo_kanban` module, and it could be at `todo_kanban/views/todo_kanban_assets.xml`:

```xml
<?xml version="1.0" encoding="utf-8"?>
<openerp>
  <data>
    <template id="assets_backend"
              inherit_id="web.assets_backend"
              name="Todo Kanban Assets" >
      <xpath expr="." position="inside">
        <link rel="stylesheet"
         href="/todo_kanban/static/src/css/todo_kanban.css"
        />
        <script type="text/javascript"
         src="/todo_kanban/static/src/js/todo_kanban.js">
        </script>
      </xpath>
    </template>
  </data>
</openerp>
```

As usual, it should be referenced in the __openerp__.py descriptor file. Notice that the assets are located inside a /static/src subdirectory. This is not required, but is a convention used in all standard modules and is the recommended practice.

Creating business reports

Reports are an important part for a business application. Since version 8, the reference report engine for Odoo is QWeb. Reports are views rendered in HTML and then exported to PDF. This means that most of what we have learned with kanban views will also be useful to design reports.

We will add a report to our module. First, we should add the file with its definition to the todo_kanban/__openerp__.py descriptor file, as shown in the following:

```
'data': ['todo_view.xml', 'todo_report.xml']
```

The todo_report.xml file can start by declaring the new report as follows:

```xml
<?xml version="1.0"?>
<openerp>
  <data>
    <report id="report_todo_task_action"
            string="To-do Tasks"
            model="todo.task"
            report_type="qweb-pdf"
            name="todo_kanban.report_todo_task_template"
    />
  </data>
</openerp>
```

The <report> tag is a shortcut to write data on the ir.actions.report.xml model, which is a particular type of client action. Their data is available in the **Settings | Technical | Reports** menu option.

After installing this, the to-do task form view will display a **Print** button at the top, at the left of before the **More** button, and a click on it will display this option to run the report.

At the moment, it won't work, since we haven't yet defined the report. This will be a QWeb report, so we will be using a QWeb template. The name attribute identifies the template to be used. Unlike other identifier references, the module prefix in the name attribute is required. We must use the full reference module_name.identifier_name.

Installing wkhtmltopdf

To correctly generate reports, a recent version of the `wkhtmltopdf` library needs to be installed. Its name stands for "Webkit HTML to PDF." Odoo uses it to convert a rendered HTML page into a PDF document.

Older versions have issues, such as not printing page headers and footers, so the `wkhtmltopdf` version should be at least 0.12.0. Unfortunately, at the time of writing, the version provided by Ubuntu is not adequate, so we need to download the latest release for your OS and CPU from `http://wkhtmltopdf.org/downloads.html`. For Ubuntu 14.04 (Trusty) 64-bit, at the time of writing this is `wkhtmltox-0.12.1_ linux-trusty-amd64.deb`.

The current version, if installed, can be checked with the following:

```
$ wkhtmltopdf --version
wkhtmltopdf 0.12.1 (with patched qt)
```

That is what we can see after installing the latest stable version at the date of writing. That's probably not what you will get now on your system. Let's go through the installation steps that will get us there.

We should make sure that the Debian/Ubuntu distributed version is not installed:

```
$ sudo apt-get remove --purge wkhtmltopdf
```

Next we should download the latest package to a temporary directory and install it:

```
$ cd /tmp
$ wget http://downloads.sourceforge.net/project/wkhtmltopdf/
archive/0.12.1/wkhtmltox-0.12.1_linux-trusty-amd64.deb
$ sudo dpkg -i wkhtmltox-0.12.1_linux-trusty-amd64.deb
```

After this, the `wkhtmltopdf` version should print out as shown previously, and the Odoo server won't display the **You need Wkhtmltopdf to print a pdf version of the report's** INFO message anymore.

QWeb report templates

The reports will usually follow a basic skeleton, as shown in the following. This can be added to the `todo_kanban/todo_report.xml` file, just after the `<report>` element.

```
<template id="report_todo_task_template">
  <t t-call="report.html_container">
    <t t-foreach="docs" t-as="o">
      <t t-call="report.external_layout">
```

```
        <div class="page">
          <!-- Report page content -->
        </div>
      </t>
    </t>
  </t>
</template>
```

The most important parts here are the `t-call` directives using standard report structures. The `report.html_container` template does the setup of supporting HTML document for us. The `report.external_layout` template handles the report header and footer, using the corresponding setup from the appropriate company. Alternatively, we can use `report.internal_layout` instead, which uses only a basic header.

Presenting data in reports

Reports also use QWeb, but they are processed server-side, using a Python QWeb engine, unlike the kanban views, which are processed client-side (in the web browser) using a JavaScript engine. You can see it as two implementations of the same specification, and there are some differences that we need to be aware of.

To start with, QWeb expressions are evaluated using Python syntax, not JavaScript. For the simplest expressions, there may be little or no difference, but more complex operations will probably be different.

The expression evaluation context is also different. For reports, we have the following variables available:

- `docs`: This is an iterable collection with the records to print
- `doc_ids`: This is a list of the IDs of the records to print
- `doc_model`: This identifies the model of the records, for example, `todo.task`
- `time`: This is a reference to Python's time library
- `user`: This is the record for the user running the report
- `res_company`: This is the record for the current user's company

The report content is written in HTML, and field values can be referenced using the `t-field` attribute, and it can be complemented with `t-field-options` to use a specific widget to render the field content.

A simple example is as follows:

```
<!-- Report page content -->
<h2 t-field="o.name" />
<p t-field="o.user_id.name" />
<ul>
  <t t-foreach="o.message_follower_ids" t-as="f">
    <li>
      <img t-if="f.image_small"
           t-att-src="'data:image/png;base64,%s' % f.image_small"
           style="max-height: 45px;" />
      <span t-field="f.name" />
    </li>
  </t>
</ul>
```

Since the rendering is done server-side, records are objects and we can use dot notation to access fields from related data.

We can also see a technique to display images stored on fields: they are automatically converted to their `base64` representation, so they can be used in a `<img src="data:..."/>` tag. This was used inside a second loop, iterating through the follower list.

Fields can be used with additional options. These are very similar to the `options` attribute used on form views, as seen in *Chapter 6, Views – Designing the User Interface*, with an additional `widget` to set the widget to use to render the field.

A common example is a monetary field, as shown in the following:

```
<span t-field="o.amount"
      t-field-options='{
         "widget": "monetary",
         "display_currency": "o.pricelist_id.currency_id"}'/>
```

A more sophisticated case is the `contact` widget, used to format addresses, as shown in the following:

```
<div t-field="res_company.partner_id"
     t-field-options='{
        "widget": "contact",
        "fields": ["address", "name", "phone", "fax"],
        "no_marker": true}' />
```

By default, some pictograms, such as a phone, are displayed in the address. The `no_marker="true"` option disables them.

Enabling language translation in reports

A helper function, `translate_doc()`, is available to dynamically translate the report content to a specific language.

It needs the name of the field where the language to use can be found. This will frequently be the Partner the document is to be sent to, usually stored at `partner_id.lang`. In our case, we don't have a Partner field, but we can use the responsible user, and the corresponding language preference is in `user_id.lang`.

The function expects a template name, and will render and translate it. This means that we need to define the page content of our report in a separate template, as shown in the following:

```
<template id="report_todo_task_template">
  <t t-call="report.html_container">
    <t t-foreach="doc_ids" t-as="doc_id">
    <t t-raw="translate_doc(doc_id, doc_model,
                            'user_id.partner_id.lang',
                            'todo_kanban.report_todo_task_doc')"/>
    </t>
  </t>
</template>
```

Designing report content

The layout of the content can be done using the Twitter Bootstrap HTML grid system. In a nutshell, Bootstrap has a grid layout with 12 columns. A new row can be added using `<div class="row">`. Inside a row, we have cells, each spanning though a certain number of columns, that should take up the 12 columns. Each cell can be defined with `<div class="col-xs-N">`, where N is the number of columns it spans.

> A complete reference for Bootstrap, describing these and other style elements, can be found at `http://getbootstrap.com/css/`.

We should now add the template for the document pages as follows:

```
<template id="report_todo_task_doc">
  <t t-call="report.external_layout">
    <div class="page">
      <div class="row">
        <div class="col-xs-12">
          <h2><span t-field="o.name" /></h2>
        </div>
```

```
        </div>
        <div class="row">
            <div class="col-xs-8">
                By: <span t-field="o.user_id" />
            </div>
            <div class="col-xs-4">
                Deadline: <span t-field="o.date_deadline" />
            </div>
        </div>
        <!-- Table -->
    </div>
  </t>
</template>
```

Here the first row spans the full page width, and the second row has two cells, taking two-thirds and one-third of the page width, respectively.

Next we will add an HTML table, at the `<!-- Table -->` comment, to display all the task followers with name and picture, as shown in the following:

```
<table class="table table-bordered">
    <!-- Table header -->
    <tr>
        <th>Avatar</th>
        <th>Name</th>
    </tr>
    <!-- Table rows -->
    <t t-foreach="o.message_follower_ids" t-as="f">
        <!-- Each row -->
        <tr>
          <td>
            <img t-if="f.image_small"
                 t-att-src="'data:image/png;base64,%s' %
                            f.image_small"
                 style="max-height: 32px;" />
          </td>
          <td>
            <span t-field="f.name"/>
          </td>
        </tr>
        <!-- Totals in a last row -->
        <t t-if="f_last">
          <tr>
            <td colspan="2">
              <strong><p class="text-right">
                <t t-esc="len(o.message_follower_ids)"/>
```

```
                          followers                              </p></
strong>
                    </td>
                  </tr>
                </t>
                <!-- End table totals -->
              </t>
          </table>
```

Here we also showed how to display a total in the last row of the table, using a `<t t-if="f_last">` block inside the loop to render the total row only on the last iteration.

Note that loop totals should not be calculated by accumulation into a variable. You will face variable scope issues, and it's also a less efficient method.

If you can't have the model give you that information (as it should, to keep the logic layer separated from the presentation layer), you should calculate those totals using Python instructions such as `len()` or `sum()`. For example, to display the total after the table:

```
<!-- Totals after the table -->
<strong><p class="text-right">
  <t t-esc="len(o.message_follower_ids )"/> followers
</p></strong>
```

Paper formats

The default paper format is defined in the company setup. But we can also specify the paper format to be used by a specific report. Unfortunately, the `<report>` tag does not support setting that, so in this case, we need to use a `<record>` instead, as shown in the following:

```
<record id="report_todo_task_action"
        model="ir.actions.report.xml">
  <field name="name">To-do Tasks</field>
  <field name="model">todo.task</field>
  <field name="report_type">qweb-html</field>
  <field name="template_name">
      todo_kanban.report_todo_task_template</field>
  <field name="paper_format_id"
          ref="report.paperformat_euro" />
</record>
```

The paper formats available are defined in **Settings | Technical | Reports | Paper Format**.

Summary

You learned about kanban boards and how to build kanban views to implement them. We also introduced QWeb templating and how it can be used to design the kanban cards. QWeb is also the rendering engine powering the website CMS, so it's growing in importance in the Odoo toolset. Finally, you had an overview on how to create reports, also using the QWeb engine.

In the next chapter, we will explore how to leverage the RPC API to interact with Odoo from external applications.

9

External API – Integration with Other Systems

Until now, we have been working with server-side code. However, the Odoo server also provides an external API, which is used by its web client and is also available for other client applications.

In this chapter, we will learn how to use the Odoo external API from our own client programs. For simplicity, we will focus on Python-based clients.

Setting up a Python client

The Odoo API can be accessed externally using two different protocols: XML-RPC and JSON-RPC. Any external program capable of implementing a client for one of these protocols will be able to interact with an Odoo server. To avoid introducing additional programming languages, we will keep using Python to explore the external API.

Until now, we have been running Python code only on the server. This time, we will use Python on the client side, so it's possible you might need to do some additional setup on your workstation.

To follow the examples in this chapter, you will need to be able to run Python files on your work computer. The Odoo server requires Python 2, but our RPC client can be in any language, so Python 3 will be just fine. However, since some readers may be running the server on the same machine they are working on (hello Ubuntu users!), it will be simpler for everyone to follow if we stick to Python 2.

If you are using Ubuntu or a Macintosh, probably Python is already installed. Open a terminal console, type `python`, and you should be greeted with something like the following:

```
Python 2.7.8 (default, Oct 20 2014, 15:05:29)
[GCC 4.9.1] on linux2
Type "help", "copyright","", "credits" or "license" for more information.
>>>
```

 Windows users can find an installer and also quickly get up to speed. The official installation packages can be found at https://www.python.org/downloads/.

Calling the Odoo API using XML-RPC

The simplest method to access the server is using XML-RPC. We can use the `xmlrpclib` library from Python's standard library for this. Remember that we are programming a client in order to connect to a server, so we need an Odoo server instance running to connect to. In our examples, we will assume that an Odoo server instance is running on the same machine (`localhost`), but you can use any IP address or server name, if the server is running on another machine.

Opening an XML-RPC connection

Let's get a fist contact with the external API. Start a Python console and type the following:

```
>>> import xmlrpclib
>>> srv, db = 'http://localhost:8069', 'v8dev'
>>> user, pwd = 'admin', 'admin'
>>> common = xmlrpclib.ServerProxy('%s/xmlrpc/2/common' % srv)
>>> common.version()
{'server_version_info': [8, 0, 0, 'final', 0], 'server_serie':
'8.0', 'server_version': '8.0', 'protocol_version': 1}
```

Here, we import the `xmlrpclib` library and then set up some variables with the information for the server location and connection credentials. Feel free to adapt these to your specific setup.

Next, we set up access to the server's public services (not requiring a login), exposed at the `/xmlrpc/2/common` endpoint. One of the methods that are available is `version()`, which inspects the server version. We use it to confirm that we can communicate with the server.

Another public method is `authenticate()`. In fact, this does not create a session, as you might be led to believe. This method just confirms that the username and password are accepted and returns the user ID that should be used in requests instead of the username, as shown here:

```
>>> uid = common.authenticate(db, user, pwd, {})
>>> print uid
1
```

Reading data from the server

With XML-RPC, no session is maintained and the authentication credentials are sent with every request. This adds some overhead to the protocol, but makes it simpler to use.

Next, we set up access to the server methods that need a login to be accessed. These are exposed at the `/xmlrpc/2/object` endpoint, as shown in the following:

```
>>> api = xmlrpclib.ServerProxy('%s/xmlrpc/2/object' % srv)
>>> api.execute_kw(db, uid, pwd, 'res.partner', 'search_count', [[]])
70
```

Here, we are doing our first access to the server API, performing a count on the Partner records. Methods are called using the `execute_kw()` method that takes the following arguments:

- The name of the database to connect to
- The connection user ID
- The user password
- The target model identifier name
- The method to call
- A list of positional arguments
- An optional dictionary with keyword arguments

The preceding example calls the `search_count` method of the `res.partner` model with one positional argument, `[]`, and no keyword arguments. The positional argument is a search domain; since we are providing an empty list, it counts all the Partners.

Frequent actions are search and read. When called from the RPC, the search method returns a list of IDs matching a domain. The browse method is not available from the RPC, and read should be used in its place to, given a list of record IDs, retrieve their data, as shown in the following code:

```
>>> api.execute_kw(db, uid, pwd, 'res.partner', 'search',
[[('country_id', '=', 'be'), ('parent_id', '!=', False)]])
[43, 42]
>>> api.execute_kw(db, uid, pwd, 'res.partner', 'read',  [[43]],
{'fields': ['id', 'name', 'parent_id']})
[{'parent_id': [7, 'Agrolait'], 'id': 43, 'name': 'Michel
Fletcher'}]
```

Note that for the read method, we are using one positional argument for the list of IDs, [43], and one keyword argument, fields. We can also notice that relational fields are retrieved as a pair, with the related record's ID and display name. That's something to keep in mind when processing the data in your code.

The search and read combination is so frequent that a search_read method is provided to perform both operations in a single step. The same result as the previous two steps can be obtained with the following:

```
>>> api.execute_kw(db, uid, pwd, 'res.partner', 'search_read',
[[('country_id', '=', 'be'), ('parent_id', '!=', False)]],
{'fields': ['id', 'name', 'parent_id']})
```

The search_read method behaves like read, but expects as first positional argument a domain instead of a list of IDs. It's worth mentioning that the field argument on read and search_read is not mandatory. If not provided, all fields will be retrieved.

Calling other methods

The remaining model methods are all exposed through RPC, except for those starting with "_" that are considered private. This means that we can use create, write, and unlink to modify data on the server as follows:

```
>>> api.execute_kw(db, uid, pwd, 'res.partner', 'create', [{'name':
'Packt'}])
75
>>> api.execute_kw(db, uid, pwd, 'res.partner', 'write', [[75],
{'name': 'Packt Pub'}])
True
>>> api.execute_kw(db, uid, pwd, 'res.partner', 'read', [[75], ['id',
'name']])
[{'id': 75, 'name': 'Packt Pub'}]
>>> api.execute_kw(db, uid, pwd, 'res.partner', 'unlink', [[75]])
True
```

One limitation of the XML-RPC protocol is that it does not support None values. The implication is that methods that don't return anything won't be usable through XML-RPC, since they are implicitly returning None. This is why methods should always finish with at least a `return True` statement.

Writing a Notes desktop application

Let's do something interesting with the RPC API. What if users could manage their Odoo to-do tasks directly from their computer's desktop? Let's write a simple Python application to do just that, as shown in the following screenshot:

For clarity, we will split it into two files: one concerned to interact with the server backend, `note_api.py`, and another with the graphical user interface, `note_gui.py`.

Communication layer with Odoo

We will create a class to set up the connection and store its information. It should expose two methods: `get()` to retrieve task data and `set()` to create or update tasks.

Select a directory to host the application files and create the `note_api.py` file. We can start by adding the class constructor, as follows:

```python
import xmlrpclib
class NoteAPI():
    def __init__(self, srv, db, user, pwd):
        common = xmlrpclib.ServerProxy(
            '%s/xmlrpc/2/common' % srv)
        self.api = xmlrpclib.ServerProxy(
            '%s/xmlrpc/2/object' % srv)
        self.uid = common.authenticate(db, user, pwd, {})
        self.pwd = pwd
        self.db = db
        self.model = 'todo.task'
```

Here we store in the created object all the information needed to execute calls on a model: the API reference, `uid`, password, database name, and the model to use.

Next we will define a helper method to execute the calls. It takes advantage of the object stored data to provide a smaller function signature, as shown next:

```python
def execute(self, method, arg_list, kwarg_dict=None):
    return self.api.execute_kw(
        self.db, self.uid, self.pwd, self.model,
        method, arg_list, kwarg_dict or {})
```

Now we can use it to implement the higher level `get()` and `set()` methods.

The `get()` method will accept an optional list of IDs to retrieve. If none are listed, all records will be returned, as shown here:

```python
def get(self, ids=None):
    domain = [('id',' in', ids)] if ids else []
    fields = ['id', 'name']
    return self.execute('search_read', [domain, fields])
```

The `set()` method will have as arguments the task text to write, and an optional ID. If ID is not provided, a new record will be created. It returns the ID of the record written or created, as shown here:

```python
def set(self, text, id=None):
    if id:
```

```
                self.execute('write', [[id], {'name': text}])
            else:
                vals = {'name': text, 'user_id': self.uid}
                id = self.execute('create', [vals])
            return id
```

Let's end the file with a small piece of test code that will be executed if we run the Python file:

```
if __name__ == '__main__':
    srv, db = 'http://localhost:8069', 'v8dev'
    user, pwd = 'admin', 'admin'
    api = NoteAPI(srv, db, user, pwd)
    from pprint import pprint
    pprint(api.get())
```

If we run the Python script, we should see the content of our to-do tasks printed out. Now that we have a simple wrapper around our Odoo backend, let's deal with the desktop user interface.

Creating the GUI

Our goal here was to learn to write the interface between an external application and the Odoo server, and this was done in the previous section. But it would be a shame not going the extra step and actually making it available to the end user.

To keep the setup as simple as possible, we will use Tkinter to implement the graphical user interface. Since it is part of the standard library, it does not require any additional installation. It is not our goal to explain how Tkinter works, so we will be short on explanations about it.

Each Task should have a small yellow window on the desktop. These windows will have a single Text widget. Pressing *Ctrl + N* will open a new Note, and pressing *Ctrl + S* will write the content of the current note to the Odoo server.

Now, alongside the note_api.py file, create a new note_gui.py file. It will first import the Tkinter modules and widgets we will use, and then the NoteAPI class, as shown in the following:

```
from Tkinter import Text, Tk
import tkMessageBox
from note_api import NoteAPI
```

Next we create our own Text widget derived from the Tkinter one. When creating an instance, it will expect an API reference, to use for the save action, and also the Task's text and ID, as shown in the following:

```
class NoteText(Text):
    def __init__(self, api, text='', id=None):
        self.master = Tk()
        self.id = id
        self.api = api
        Text.__init__(self, self.master, bg='#f9f3a9',
                      wrap='word', undo=True)
        self.bind('<Control-n>', self.create)
        self.bind('<Control-s>', self.save)
        if id:
            self.master.title('#%d' % id)
        self.delete('1.0', 'end')
        self.insert('1.0', text)
        self.master.geometry('220x235')
        self.pack(fill='both', expand=1)
```

The `Tk()` constructor creates a new UI window and the Text widget places itself inside it, so that creating a new `NoteText` instance automatically opens a desktop window.

Next, we will implement the `create` and `save` actions. The `create` action opens a new empty window, but it will be stored in the server only when a `save` action is performed, as shown in the following code:

```
def create(self, event=None):
    NoteText(self.api, '')
def save(self, event=None):
    text = self.get('1.0', 'end')
    self.id = self.api.set(text, self.id)
    tkMessageBox.showinfo('Info', 'Note %d Saved.' % self.id)
```

The `save` action can be performed either on existing or on new tasks, but there is no need to worry about that here since those cases are already handled by the `set()` method of `NoteAPI`.

Finally, we will add the code that retrieves and creates all note windows when the program is started, as shown in the following code:

```
if __name__ == '__main__':
    srv, db = 'http://localhost:8069', 'v8dev'
    user, pwd = 'admin', 'admin'
    api = NoteAPI(srv, db, user, pwd)
    for note in api.get():
        x = NoteText(api, note['name'], note['id'])
    x.master.mainloop()
```

The last command runs `mainloop()` on the last Note window created, to start waiting for window events.

This is a very basic application, but the point here is to make an example of interesting ways to leverage the Odoo RPC API.

Introducing the ERPpeek client

ERPpeek is a versatile tool that can be used both as an interactive **Command-line Interface (CLI)** and as a **Python library**, with a more convenient API than the one provided by `xmlrpclib`. It is available from the PyPi index and can be installed with the following:

```
$ pip install -U erppeek
```

On a Unix system, if you are installing it system wide, you might need to prepend `sudo` to the command.

The ERPpeek API

The `erppeek` library provides a programming interface, wrapping around `xmlrpclib`, which is similar to the programming interface we have for the server-side code.

Our point here is to provide a glimpse of what `ERPpeek` has to offer, and not to provide a full explanation of all its features.

We can start by reproducing our first steps with `xmlrpclib` using `erppeek` as follows:

```
>>> import erppeek
>>> api = erppeek.Client('http://localhost:8069', 'v8dev',
    'admin', 'admin')
>>> api.common.version()
>>> api.count('res.partner', [])
>>> api.search('res.partner', [('country_id', '=', 'be'),
    ('parent_id', '!=', False)])
>>> api.read('res.partner', [43], ['id', 'name', 'parent_id'])
```

As you can see, the API calls use fewer arguments and are similar to the server-side counterparts.

But `ERPpeek` doesn't stop here, and also provides a representation for Models. We have the following two alternative ways to get an instance for a model, either using the `model()` method or accessing an attribute in camel case:

```
>>> m = api.model('res.partner')
>>> m = api.ResPartner
```

Now we can perform actions on that model as follows:

```
>>> m.count([('name', 'like', 'Packt%')])
1
>>> m.search([('name', 'like', 'Packt%')])
[76]
```

It also provides client-side object representation for records as follows:

```
>>> recs = m.browse([('name', 'like', 'Packt%')])
>>> recs
<RecordList 'res.partner, [76]'>
>>> recs.name
['Packt']
```

As you can see, `ERPpeek` goes a long way from plain `xmlrpclib`, and makes it possible to write code that can be reused server side with little or no modification.

The ERPpeek CLI

Not only can `erppeek` be used as a Python library, it is also a CLI that can be used to perform administrative actions on the server. Where the `odoo shell` command provided a local interactive session on the host server, `erppeek` provides a remote interactive session on a client across the network.

Opening a command line, we can have a peek at the options available, as shown in the following:

```
$ erppeek --help
```

Let's see a sample session as follows:

```
$ erppeek --server='http://localhost:8069' -d v8dev -u admin
Usage (some commands):
    models(name)                    # List models matching pattern
    model(name)                     # Return a Model instance
(...)
```

```
Password for 'admin':
Logged in as 'admin'
v8dev >>> model('res.users').count()
3
v8dev >>> rec = model('res.partner').browse(43)
v8dev >>> rec.name
'Michel Fletcher'
```

As you can see, a connection was made to the server, and the execution context provided a reference to the model() method to get model instances and perform actions on them.

The erppeek.Client instance used for the connection is also available through the client variable. Notably, it provides an alternative to the web client to manage the following modules installed:

- client.modules(): This can search and list modules available or installed
- client.install(): This performs module installation
- client.upgrade(): This orders modules to be upgraded
- client.uninstall(): This uninstalls modules

So, ERPpeek can also provide good service as a remote administration tool for Odoo servers.

Summary

Our goal for this chapter was to learn how the external API works and what it is capable of. We started exploring it using a simple Python XML-RPC client, but the external API can be used from any programming language. In fact, the official docs provide code examples for Java, PHP, and Ruby.

There are a number of libraries to handle XML-RPC or JSON-RPC, some generic and some specific for use with Odoo. We tried not point out any libraries in particular, except for erppeek, since it is not only a proven wrapper for the Odoo/OpenERP XML-RPC but because it is also an invaluable tool for remote server management and inspection.

Until now, we used our Odoo server instances for development and tests. But to have a production grade server, there are additional security and optimization configurations that need to be done. In the next chapter, we will focus on them.

10

Deployment Checklist – Going Live

In this chapter, you will learn how to prepare your Odoo server for use in the production environment.

There are many possible strategies and tools that can be used to deploy and manage an Odoo production server. We will guide you through one way of doing it.

This is the server setup checklist that we will follow:

- Install Odoo from the source
- Set up the Odoo configuration file
- Set up multiprocessing workers
- Set up the Odoo system service
- Set up a reverse proxy with SSL support

Let's get started.

Installing Odoo

Odoo has Debian/Ubuntu packages available for installation. With these, you get a working server process that automatically starts on system boot. This installation process is straightforward, and you can find all you need at http://nightly.odoo.com.

While this is an easy and convenient way to install Odoo, here we prefer running from version-controlled source code since this provides better control over what is deployed.

Installing from the source code

Sooner or later, your server will need upgrades and patches. A version controlled repository can be of great help when the time comes.

We use `git` to get our code from a repository, just like we did to install the development environment. For example:

```
$ git clone https://github.com/odoo/odoo.git -b 8.0 --depth=1
```

This command gets from GitHub the branch 8.0 source code into an `odoo/` subdirectory. At the time of writing, 8.0 is the default branch, so the `-b 8.0` option is optional. The `--depth=1` option was used to get a shallow copy of the repository, without all version history. This reduces the disk space used and makes the clone operation much faster.

It might be worthwhile to have a slightly more sophisticated setup, with a staging environment alongside the production environment.

With this, we could fetch the latest source code version and test it in the staging environment, without disturbing the production environment. When we're happy with the new version, we would deploy it from staging to production.

Let's consider the repository at `~/odoo-dev/odoo` to be our staging environment. It was cloned from GitHub, so that a `git pull` inside it will fetch and merge the latest changes. But it is also a repository itself, and we can clone it for our production environment, as shown in the following example:

```
$ mkdir ~/odoo-prd && cd ~/odoo-prd
$ git clone ~/odoo-dev/odoo ~/odoo-prd/odoo/
```

This will create the production repository at `~/odoo-prd/odoo` cloned from the staging `~/odoo-dev/odoo`. It will be set to track that repository, so that a git pull inside production will fetch and merge the last versions from staging. Git is smart enough to know that this is a local clone and uses hard links to the parent repository to save disk space, so the `--depth` option is unnecessary.

Whenever a problem found in production needs troubleshooting, we can checkout in the staging environment the version of the production code, and then debug to diagnose and solve the issue, without touching the production code. Later, the solution patch can be committed to the staging Git history, and then deployed to the production repository using a `git pull` command on it.

Git will surely be an invaluable tool to manage the versions of your Odoo deployments. We just scratched the surface of what can be done to manage code versions. If you're not already familiar with Git, it's worth learning more about it. A good starting point is `http://git-scm.com/doc`.

Setting up the configuration file

Adding the `--save` option when starting an Odoo server saves the configuration used to the `~/.openerp_serverrc` file. We can use the file as a starting point for our server configuration, which will be stored on `/etc/odoo`, as shown in the following code:

```
$ sudo mkdir /etc/odoo
$ sudo chown $(whoami) /etc/odoo
$ cp ~/.openerp_serverrc /etc/odoo/openerp-server.conf
```

This will have the configuration parameters to be used by our server instance.

The following are the parameters essential for the server to work correctly:

- `addons_path`: This is a comma-separated list of the paths where modules will be looked up, using the directories from left to right. This means that the leftmost directories in the list have a higher priority.
- `xmlrpc_port`: This is the port number at which the server will listen. By default, port 8069 is used.
- `log_level`: This is the log verbosity. The default is the `info` level, but using the `debug_rpc` level, while more verbose, adds important information to monitor server performance.

The following settings are also important for a production instance:

- `admin_passwd`: This is the master password to access the web client database management functions. It's critical to set this with a strong password or an empty value to deactivate the function.
- `dbfilter`: This is a Python-interpreted regex expression to filter the databases to be listed. For the user to not be prompted to select a database, it should be set with `^dbname$`, for example, `dbfilter = ^v8dev$`.
- `logrotate=True`: This will split the log into daily files and keep only one month of log history.
- `data_dir`: This is the path where the attachment files are stored. Remember to have backups on it.
- `without_demo=True`: This should be set in production environments so that new databases do not have demo data on them.

When using a reverse proxy, the following settings should be considered:

- `proxy_mode=True`: This is important to set when using a reverse proxy.
- `xmlrpc-interface`: This sets the addresses that will be listened to. By default, it listens to all `0.0.0.0`, but when using a reverse proxy, it can be set to `127.0.0.1` in order to respond only to local requests.

A production instance is expected to handle significant workload. By default, the server runs one process and is capable of handling only one request at a time. However, a multiprocess mode is available so that concurrent requests can be handled. The option `workers=N` sets the number of worker processes to use. As a guideline, you can try setting it to `1+2*P`, where `P` is the number of processors. The best setting to use needs to be tuned for each case, since it depends on the server load and what other services are running on the server (such as PostgreSQL).

We can check the effect of the settings made by running the server with the `-c` or `--config` option as follows:

```
$ ./odoo.py -c /etc/odoo/openerp-server.conf
```

Setting up as a system service

Next, we will want to set up Odoo as a system service and have it started automatically when the system boots.

The Odoo source code includes an init script, used for the Debian packaged distribution. We can use it as our service init script with minor modifications as follows:

```
$ sudo cp ~/odoo-prd/odoo/debian/init /etc/init.d/odoo
$ sudo chmod +x /etc/init.d/odoo
```

At this point, you might want to check the content of the init script. The key parameters are assigned to variables at the top of the file. A sample is as follows:

```
PATH=/sbin:/bin:/usr/sbin:/usr/bin:/usr/local/bin
DAEMON=/usr/bin/openerp-server
NAME=odoo
DESC=odoo
CONFIG=/etc/odoo/openerp-server.conf
LOGFILE=/var/log/odoo/odoo-server.log
PIDFILE=/var/run/${NAME}.pid
USER=odoo
```

The USER variable is the system user under which the server will run, and you probably want to change it. The other variables should be adequate and we will prepare the rest of the setup having their default values in mind. DAEMON is the path to the server executable, CONFIG is the configuration file to use, and LOGFILE is the log file location.

The DAEMON executable can be a symbolic link to our actual Odoo location, as shown in the following:

```
$ sudo ln -s ~/odoo-prd/odoo/odoo.py /usr/bin/openerp-server
$ sudo chown $(whoami) /usr/bin/openerp-server
```

Next we must create the LOGFILE directory as follows:

```
$ sudo mkdir /var/log/odoo
$ sudo chown $(whoami) /etc/odoo
```

Now we should be able to start and stop our Odoo service as follows:

```
$ sudo /etc/init.d/odoo start
Starting odoo: ok
```

We should now be able to get a response from the server and see no errors in the log file, as shown in the following:

```
$ curl http://localhost:8069
<html><head><script>window.location = '/web' +
location.hash;</script></head></html>
$ less /var/log/odoo/odoo-server.log   # show the log file
```

Stopping the service is done in a similar way, as shown in the following:

```
$ sudo /etc/init.d/odoo stop
Stopping odoo: ok
```

 Ubuntu provides the easier to remember service command to manage services. If you prefer, you can instead use sudo service odoo start and sudo service odoo stop.

We now only need to make this service start automatically on system boot:

```
$ sudo update-rc.d odoo defaults
```

After this, when we reboot our server, the Odoo service should be started automatically and with no errors. It's a good time to check that all is working as expected.

Using a reverse proxy

While Odoo itself can serve web pages, it is strongly recommended to have a reverse proxy in front of it. A reverse proxy acts as an intermediary managing the traffic between the clients sending requests and the Odoo servers responding to them. Using a reverse proxy has several benefits.

On the security side, it can do the following:

- Handle (and enforce) HTTPS protocols to encrypt traffic
- Hide the internal network characteristics
- Act an "application firewall" limiting the URLs accepted for processing

And on the performance side, it can provide significant improvements:

- Cache static content, thus reducing the load on the Odoo servers
- Compress content to speed up loading times
- Act as a load balancer distributing load between several servers

Apache is a popular option to use as reverse proxy. Nginx is a recent alternative with good technical arguments. Here we will choose to use nginx as a reverse proxy and show how it can be used perform the functions mentioned above.

Setting up nginx for reverse proxy

First, we should install nginx. We want it to listen on the default HTTP ports, so we should make sure they are not already taken by some other service. Performing this command should result in an error, as shown in the following:

```
$ curl http://localhost
curl: (7) Failed to connect to localhost port 80
```

If not, you should disable or remove that service to allow nginx to use those ports. For example, to stop an existing Apache server you should:

```
$ sudo /etc/init.d/apache2 stop
```

Now we can install nginx, which is done in the expected way:

```
$ sudo apt-get install nginx
```

To confirm that it is working correctly, we should see a "Welcome to nginx" page when visiting the server address with a browser or using `curl http://localhost` in the server.

Nginx configuration files follow the same approach as Apache: they are stored in `/etc/nginx/available-sites/` and activated by adding a symbolic link in `/etc/nginx/enabled-sites/`. We should also disable the default configuration provided by the nginx installation, as shown in the following:

```
$ sudo rm /etc/nginx/sites-enabled/default
```

```
$ sudo touch /etc/nginx/sites-available/odoo
```

```
$ sudo ln -s
/etc/nginx/sites-available/odoo /etc/nginx/sites-enabled/odoo
```

Using an editor, such as nano or vi, we should edit our nginx configuration file as follows:

```
$ sudo nano /etc/nginx/sites-available/odoo
```

First we add the upstreams, the backend servers nginx will redirect traffic to, the Odoo server in our case, which is listening on port 8069, shown in the following:

```
upstream backend-odoo {
    server 127.0.0.1:8069;
}
server {
    location / {
        proxy_pass http://backend-odoo;
    }
}
```

To test if the edited configuration is correct, use the following:

```
$ sudo nginx -t
```

In case you find errors, confirm the configuration file is correctly typed. Also, a common problem is for the default HTTP to be taken by another service, such as Apache or the default nginx website. Double-check the instructions given before to make sure that this is not the case, then restart nginx. After this, we can have nginx to reload the new configuration as follows:

```
$ sudo /etc/init.d/nginx reload
```

We can now confirm that nginx is redirecting traffic to the backend Odoo server, as shown in the following:

```
$ curl http://localhost
<html><head><script>window.location = '/web' +
location.hash;</script></head></html>
```

Enforcing HTTPS

Next we should install a certificate to be able to use SSL. To create a self-signed certificate, follow the following steps:

```
$ sudo mkdir /etc/nginx/ssl && cd /etc/nginx/ssl
$ sudo openssl req -x509
-newkey rsa:2048 -keyout key.pem -out cert.pem -days 365 -nodes
$ sudo chmod a-wx *            # make files read only
$ sudo chown www-data:root *   # access only to www-data group
```

This creates an `ssl/` directory inside the `/etc/nginx/` directory and creates a password less self-signed SSL certificate. When running the `openssl` command, some additional information will be asked, and a certificate and key files are generated. Finally, the ownership of these files is given to the user `www-data` used to run the web server.

> Using self-signed certificated can pose some security risks, such as man-in-the-middle attacks, and may even not be allowed by some browsers. For a robust solution, you should use a certificate signed by a recognized certificate authority. This is particularly important if you are running a commercial or e-commerce website.

Now that we have an SSL certificate, we are ready to configure nginx to use it.

To enforce HTTPS, we will redirect all HTTP traffic to it. Replace the `server` directive we defined previously with the following:

```
server {
  listen 80;
  add_header Strict-Transport-Security max-age=2592000;
  rewrite ^/.*$ https://$host$request_uri? permanent;
}
```

If we reload the nginx configuration now and access the server with a web browser, we will see that the `http://` address will be converted into an `https://` address.

But it won't return any content before we configure the HTTPS service properly, by adding the following server configuration:

```
server {
  listen 443 default;
  # ssl settings
  ssl on;
```

```
    ssl_certificate        /etc/nginx/ssl/cert.pem;
    ssl_certificate_key /etc/nginx/ssl/key.pem;
    keepalive_timeout 60;
    # proxy header and settings
    proxy_set_header Host $host;
    proxy_set_header X-Real-IP $remote_addr;
    proxy_set_header X-Forward-For $proxy_add_x_forwarded_for;
    proxy_set_header X-Forwarded-Proto $scheme;
    proxy_redirect off;

    location / {
      proxy_pass http://backend-odoo;
    }
  }
```

This will listen to the HTTPS port and use the /etc/nginx/ssl/ certificate files to encrypt the traffic. We also add some information to the request header to let the Odoo backend service know it's being proxied. For security reasons, it's important for Odoo to make sure the proxy_mode parameter is set to True. At the end, the location directive defines that all request are passed to the backend-odoo upstream.

Reload the configuration, and we should have our Odoo service working through HTTPS, as shown in the following:

```
$ sudo nginx -t
nginx: the configuration file /etc/nginx/nginx.conf syntax is ok
nginx: configuration file /etc/nginx/nginx.conf test is successful
$ sudo service nginx reload
 * Reloading nginx configuration nginx
    ...done.
$ curl -k https://localhost
<html><head><script>window.location = '/web' +
location.hash;</script></head></html>
```

The last output confirms that the Odoo web client is being served over HTTPS.

Nginx optimizations

Now, it is time for some fine-tuning of the nginx settings. They are recommended to enable response buffering and data compression that should improve the speed of the website. We also set a specific location for the logs.

The following configurations should be added inside the server listening on port 443, for example, just after the proxy definitions:

```
# odoo log files
access_log /var/log/nginx/odoo-access.log;
error_log  /var/log/nginx/odoo-error.log;
# increase proxy buffer size
proxy_buffers 16 64k;
proxy_buffer_size 128k;
# force timeouts if the backend dies
proxy_next_upstream error timeout invalid_header http_500
http_502 http_503;
# enable data compression
gzip on;
gzip_min_length 1100;
gzip_buffers 4 32k;
gzip_types text/plain application/x-javascript text/xml text/css;
gzip_vary on;
```

We can also activate static content caching for faster responses to the types of requests mentioned in the preceding code example and to avoid their load on the Odoo server. After the `location /` section, add the following second location section:

```
location ~* /web/static/ {
  # cache static data
  proxy_cache_valid 200 60m;
  proxy_buffering on;
  expires 864000;
  proxy_pass http://backend-odoo;
}
```

With this, the static data is cached for 60 minutes. Further requests on those requests in that interval will be responded to directly by nginx from the cache.

Long polling

Long polling is used to support the instant messaging app, and when using multiprocessing workers, it is handled on a separate port, which is 8072 by default.

For our reverse proxy, this means that the longpolling requests should be passed to this port. To support this, we need to add a new upstream to our nginx configuration, as shown in the following code:

```
upstream backend-odoo-im { server 127.0.0.1:8072; }
```

Next, we should add another location to the server handling the HTTPS requests, as shown in the following code:

```
location /longpolling { proxy_pass http://backend-odoo-im; }
```

With these settings, nginx should pass these requests to the proper Odoo server port.

Server and module updates

Once the Odoo server is ready and running, there will come a time when you need to install updates on Odoo. This involves two steps: first, to get the new versions of the source code (server or modules), and second, to install them.

If you have followed the approach described in the *Installing from the source code* section, we can fetch and test the new versions in the staging repository. It is strongly advised that you make a copy of the production database and test the upgrade on it. If v8dev were our production database, this could be done with the following commands:

```
$ dropdb v8test ; createdb v8test
$ pg_dump v8dev | psql -d v8test
$ cd ~/odoo-dev/odoo/
$ ./odoo.py -d v8test --xmlrpc-port=8080 -c
/etc/odoo/openerp-server.conf -u all
```

If everything goes OK, it should be safe to perform the upgrade on the production service. Remember to make a note of the current version Git reference, in order to be able to roll back by checking out this version again. Keeping a backup of the database before performing the upgrade is also highly advised.

After this, we can pull the new versions to the production repository using Git and complete the upgrade, as shown here:

```
$ cd ~/odoo-prd/odoo/
$ git pull
$ ./odoo.py -c /etc/odoo/openerp-server.conf
--stop-after-init -d v8dev -u all
$ sudo /etc/init.d/odoo restart
```

Summary

In this chapter, you learned about the additional steps to set up and run Odoo in a Debian-based production server. The most important settings in the configuration file were visited, and you learned how to take advantage of the multiprocessing mode.

For improved security and scalability, you also learned how to use nginx as a reverse proxy in front of our Odoo server processes.

We hope this covers the essentials of what is needed to run an Odoo server and provide a stable and secure service to your users.

Index

A

B

C

creating 27
header status bar 94, 95

G

Gantt views
about 106
attributes 106
Git
about 173
URL 173
graph views
about 107
attributes 107
groups
used, for organizing forms 29

H

header status bar, form views
about 94, 95
business flow pipeline 95
content, organizing 98, 99
labels, for fields 96
smart buttons 97, 98
subtitle 96
tabbed notebooks 99
title 96
hierarchical relations 81
host
setting up, for Odoo server 1, 2
HTTPS
enforcing 178, 179

I

icon
adding, to modules 35
inheritance
used, for adding social network
    features 48, 49
used, for extending models 46
installation, wkhtmltopdf library 152

J

JavaScript assets
using 150

K

kanban board
about 133
example 134
kanban views 134, 135
using 134
kanban cards
about 148
colors, adding 149
option menu, adding 148, 149
text ellipsis, using 150
kanban views
about 134, 135
actions 140
card kanban view 140, 141
Custom CSS assets 150
designing 136
elements 137, 138
JavaScript assets 150
vignette kanban view 138, 139
kanban views, fields
kanban state 137
priority 137
keys, Odoo app store
category 20
license 20
summary 20
version 20
website 20

L

Linux text editor
using 10
list views
about 103
adding 30
attributes 103
long polling 180

M

many to many relations 59, 79, 80
many to one relation 59
menu entries
adding 25, 26

production instance settings, Odoo
  admin_passwd 173
  data_dir 173
  dbfilter 173
  logrotate=True 173
  without_demo=True 173
product versions, Odoo 7
prototype inheritance
  used, for copying features 46
Python classes
  models 72
Python client
  setting up 159, 160
Python debugger commands
  URL 9

Q

QWeb
  about 133
  other directives 148
QWeb, directives
  t-debug 148
  t-js 148
  t-log 148
QWeb dynamic content
  adding 141
  conditional rendering, with t-if 142
  dynamic attributes, with t-att- prefixes 144
  loop, rendering with t-foreach 143, 144
  string substitution attributes, with
    t-attf- prefixes 145
  templates, calling with t-call 146, 147
  values, rendering with t-esc 143
  values, rendering with t-raw 143
  variables, setting with t-set 145, 146
QWeb report templates
  using 152

R

recordset
  manipulating 123
  operations 124
records, in CSV data files 59, 60
related fields 85

relation fields
  many to many 117
  many to one 117
  one to many 118
  using 118
relations, models
  about 78
  hierarchical 81
  many to many 79, 80
  many to one 79
  one to many inverse 81
reserved field names 77
reverse proxy
  nginx, setting up for 176, 177
  using 176
row level access rules 34, 35

S

Samba
  configuring 10, 12
  installing 10, 12
search() method 118
search views
  about 104
  adding 30
  extending 45
  filter elements, attributes 105
Secure Shell (SSH) 2
server
  dates, working with 121, 122
  low-level SQL 120, 121
  models, querying 118, 119
  recordset operations 124
  recordsets, manipulating 123
  records, writing on 119, 120
  relation fields, using 118
  relation fields, working with 122
  time, working with 121, 122
  transactions 120, 121
  working with 116, 117
server configuration options
  about 8
  listening port, modifying 8
  logging 9
server updates 181

Thank you for buying
Odoo Development Essentials

About Packt Publishing

Packt, pronounced 'packed', published its first book, *Mastering phpMyAdmin for Effective MySQL Management*, in April 2004, and subsequently continued to specialize in publishing highly focused books on specific technologies and solutions.

Our books and publications share the experiences of your fellow IT professionals in adapting and customizing today's systems, applications, and frameworks. Our solution-based books give you the knowledge and power to customize the software and technologies you're using to get the job done. Packt books are more specific and less general than the IT books you have seen in the past. Our unique business model allows us to bring you more focused information, giving you more of what you need to know, and less of what you don't.

Packt is a modern yet unique publishing company that focuses on producing quality, cutting-edge books for communities of developers, administrators, and newbies alike. For more information, please visit our website at www.packtpub.com.

About Packt Open Source

In 2010, Packt launched two new brands, Packt Open Source and Packt Enterprise, in order to continue its focus on specialization. This book is part of the Packt Open Source brand, home to books published on software built around open source licenses, and offering information to anybody from advanced developers to budding web designers. The Open Source brand also runs Packt's Open Source Royalty Scheme, by which Packt gives a royalty to each open source project about whose software a book is sold.

Writing for Packt

We welcome all inquiries from people who are interested in authoring. Book proposals should be sent to author@packtpub.com. If your book idea is still at an early stage and you would like to discuss it first before writing a formal book proposal, then please contact us; one of our commissioning editors will get in touch with you.

We're not just looking for published authors; if you have strong technical skills but no writing experience, our experienced editors can help you develop a writing career, or simply get some additional reward for your expertise.

Working with OpenERP

ISBN: 978-1-78216-380-0   Paperback: 334 pages

Learn to utilize OpenERP to transform and streamline your business

1. Learn to install and configure OpenERP on Windows or Ubuntu.

2. Understand how to enter sales orders, create invoices, and receive payments step-by-step.

3. Implement powerful purchasing and manufacturing modules in OpenERP using real-world examples.

4. Learn advanced OpenERP features and how to create your own custom modules.

IPython Interactive Computing and Visualization Cookbook

ISBN: 978-1-78328-481-8   Paperback: 512 pages

Over 100 hands-on recipes to sharpen your skills in high-performance numerical computing and data science with Python

1. Find out how to improve your Code to write high-quality, readable, and well-tested programs with IPython.

2. Master all of the new features of the IPython Notebook, including interactive HTML/JavaScript widgets.

3. Analyze data effectively using Bayesian and Frequentist data models with Pandas, PyMC, and R.

Please check **www.PacktPub.com** for information on our titles

Administrating Solr

ISBN: 978-1-78328-325-5   Paperback: 120 pages

Master the use of Drupal and associated scripts to administrate, monitor, and optimize Solr

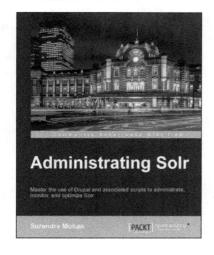

1. Learn how to work with monitoring tools like OpsView, New Relic, and SPM.

2. Utilize Solr scripts and Collection Distribution scripts to manage Solr.

3. Employ search features like querying, categorizing, search based on location, and distributed search.

Python Data Analysis

ISBN: 978-1-78355-335-8   Paperback: 348 pages

Learn how to apply powerful data analysis techniques with popular open source Python modules

1. Learn how to find, manipulate, and analyze data using Python.

2. Perform advanced, high performance linear algebra and mathematical calculations with clean and efficient Python code.

3. Explore predictive analytics and machine learning using SciKit-Learn with this Python machine learning tutorial.

4. Learn cluster and regression analysis.

Please check **www.PacktPub.com** for information on our titles